Introduction to Early Buddhism

INTRODUCTION TO EARLY BUDDHISM

An Accessible Explanation of the Core Theory of Early Buddhism

INTRODUCTION TO EARLY BUDDHISM
An Accessible Explanation of the Core Theory of Early Buddhism

The first edition in Korean: August 30, 2017
The first edition in English: August 30, 2017, December 15, 2019

AUTHOR: Bhikkhu Kakmuk
TRANSLATOR: Nancy Acord [a.k.a. Sohn, Dong Ran]
EDITOR: Mary G. Grant
COVER DESIGN: Natalie Friedemann-Weinberg
NARRATOR: Sean Slater
TYPESETTING: Raphaël Freeman MISTD, Renana Typesetting

PUBLISHER: Nibbana Buddhist Education Foundation
12606 Nieman Road Overland Park, KS 66213
www.nbef.education
nbef.book@gmail.com

ISBN 978-0-578-62306-1

Preface

It has been 26 years since I went abroad to India to study, in the hope that I would someday translate the Tipiṭaka[1] into Korean. In 2002, upon returning from India after ten years of studying the Pāli[2] and Sanskrit[3] languages, Bhikkhuni[4] Daerim and I established the Center for Early Buddhist Studies. In 2012, ten years after we started, we completed the translation of the four Nikāyas[5] – all 19 volumes.

While translating the Early Buddhist discourses, I started to think about writing a handbook for Early Buddhist theory and practice based on the Nikāyas. My wish was realized when the Saṁyutta Nikāya[6] – all six volumes – was published, ultimately resulting in the publication of *Understanding Early Buddhism* in August 2010. However, *Understanding Early Buddhism* is a vast

---

1 The Pāli word, Tipiṭaka means three baskets and is the term used for the three collections of the Early Buddhist discourses.
2 Pāli is the language most frequently used by the Buddha. The Early Buddhist discourses are written in Pāli.
3 Sanskrit is one of the languages of India.
4 Bhikkhuni is the designation for a Buddhist Nun.
5 Nikāya is the Pāli word for volume. It is frequently used for collections of the Early Buddhist discourses.
6 The Saṁyutta Nikāya [Connected Discourses] is the third of the five Nikāyas [collections] of the Pāli Tipiṭaka of Early Buddhism.

and complex commentary which may present challenges for first time readers.

This book, *Introduction to Early Buddhism*, is a response to many requests for an accessible guide to Early Buddhist teachings. The contents of this book are a compilation of a series of 50 newspaper articles published in the Bulgyo newspaper in South Korea in 2010. The purpose of this compilation was to organize the articles' content in a concise and systematic manner. I wrote this book in the hope that it would truly provide readers with an easier understanding of the core theory of Early Buddhism.

I would like to thank the editorial staff of Esol publishing for working tirelessly, planning, rewriting, and editing to make this book possible. Also, I would like to thank the rewrite team members, Dosan, Khemavati, and Suvanna at the Center for Early Buddhist Studies for correcting the original manuscript. Lastly, I dedicate this book to Bhikkhuni Daerim, the head of the Center for Early Buddhist Studies. May Bhikkhuni Daerim continue to enjoy good health and successfully finish the complete translation of the Pāli Tipiṭaka.

May all the readers of this book establish a firm foundation for deliverance·Nibbāna in this life.

September 27th, 2014
At Sil-Sang-Sha
Bhikkhu Kakmuk

TABLE OF CONTENTS

Contents

NOTES

1. Unless otherwise indicated, the Tipiṭaka and the commen-
    taries are of the Pali Text Society's edition [Ee]. The Visud-
    dhimagga [the Path of Purification] is of the HOS edition.

    For example, S12:15 is the 15th discourse of 12th Saṁyutta of
    the Saṁyutta Nikāya, and DA.i.104 is page 104 of volume 1 of the
    Dīgha Nikāya[1] commentary. Except for the sub-commentary of
    the Dīgha Nikāya, all other sub-commentaries are of the Sixth
    Buddhist Council held in Myanmar [Be] [Chaṭṭhasaṅgāyana
    edition].

2. ( ) is used after a quotation for source citation and [ ] is used
    for supplementary information.

3. Center of Early Buddhist Studies is also known as the Center
    for Early Buddhist Studies.

---

1 The Dīgha Nikāya [Collection of Long Discourses] is the first of the five
Nikāyas.

ABBREVIATIONS

A.   Aṅguttara Nikāya
AA.   Aṅguttara Nikāya Aṭṭhakathā=Manorathapūraṇī

CBETA CBETA Chinese Electronic Tripitaka Collection:
        CD-ROM

D.   Dīgha Nikāya
DA.   Dīgha Nikāya Aṭṭhakathā=Sumaṅgalavilāsnī
Dhp.   Dhammapada
Dhs.   Dhammasaṅgaṇi
DhsA.   Dhammasaṅgaṇi Aṭṭhakathā=Aṭṭhasālinī

ItA.   Itivuttaka Aṭṭhakathā

M.   Majjhima Nikāya
MA.   Majjhima Nikāya Aṭṭhakathā
MAṬ.   Majjhima Nikāya Aṭṭhakathā Ṭīkā

PED   Pāli-English Dictionary [PTS]
Pm.   Paramatthamañjūsā=Visuddhimagga Mahāṭīkā
Ps.   Paṭisambhidāmagga
PsA.   Paṭisambhidāmagga Aṭṭakathā
PTS   Pāli Text Society

S.   Saṁyutta Nikāya
SA.   Saṁyutta Nikāya Aṭṭhakathā=Sāratthappakāsinī

Sk.	Sanskrit
Sn.	Suttanipāta

ThagA.	Theragāthā Aṭṭhakathā

Ud.	Udāna
UdA.	Udāna Aṭṭhakathā

Vbh.	Vibhaṅga
Vin.	Vinaya Piṭaka
Vis.	Visuddhimagga

The Summary Outline
of Early Buddhism

CHAPTER 1

What is Early Buddhism?

Primitive, Fundamental, or Early Buddhism?

Buddhism is based on teachings of the Buddha. So, who is the Buddha? Toward the end of the 19th century, there were many opinions among western scholars as to whether or not the Buddha existed. However, around 1905, when the Emperor Ashoka's stone pillar with inscriptions was discovered in Lumbini, a place known as the birthplace of the Buddha, these controversies ended. The inscriptions engraved on the pillar are the five lines made up of 93 Ashokan characters, among which are the following:

Hida Budhe jāte Sākyamuni
Here was born Buddha, the sage of the Sākyans.

This third century BC engraved sentence on the Ashokan pillar is clear evidence showing that the Buddha existed in person.

Buddhism's 2,600-year history starts with Sākyamuni Buddha, the person named Gautama Siddhārtha. All schools of Buddhism that followed are rooted in his 45 years of teaching.

The Buddhist scholars around the world classify Buddhism's 2600-year journey into eight broad categories: Abhidhamma

[Abhidharma], Mādhyamaka, Yogācāra, Tathāgata-garbha, Pure Land, Esoteric, Seon, and Early Buddhism. If we were to imagine the whole of Buddhism as a tree, Early Buddhism would be the roots of the tree, Abhidhamma [Abhidharma] would be the trunk of the tree, Mādhyamaka, Yogācāra, Tathāgata-garbha, Pure Land, Esoteric, and Seon Buddhism would be the leaves of the tree.

Therefore, Early Buddhism is the foundation of all Buddhism. Just as a tree cannot live without its roots, later Buddhism could not exist without the Buddha's authentic voice. The precedence of Early Buddhism is indisputable, since the history of Buddhism has been well verified through proper documentation and research.

So, what is Early Buddhism? Early Buddhism is following the original teaching of the Buddha and his direct disciples. Subsequent to the Buddha's passing, the rules of conduct were recited by the Venerable Upāli[1] and compiled as the *Collection of Rules of Conduct* [the Vinaya-Piṭaka]. Dhamma was memorized by the Venerable Ānanda[2] and compiled as the *Collection of Discourses* [the Sutta-Piṭaka].

Early Buddhism is grounded in the teachings of the Pāli Tipiṭaka – the five volumes of the *Collection of Rules of Conduct*, the five Nikāyas of the *Collection of Discourses*, and the seven volumes of the Abhidhamma.[3] Historically, the Nikāyas of Southern Theravada Buddhism and the *Āgama Discourse* [Chinese translation] of Northern Buddhism are the clear authorities of Early Buddhism.

Therefore, the importance of Early Buddhist discourses that contain the Buddha's original teaching cannot be overstated. This is why modern Buddhist scholars like Dr. Mastani Fumio of Japan have emphasized the fact that Buddhism has been introduced

---

1 The Venerable Upāli is one of the ten principal direct disciples of the Buddha.
2 The Venerable Ānanda is one of the ten principal direct disciples of the Buddha.
3 The Abhidhamma is a detailed scholastic reworking of material appearing in the Early Buddhist discourses.

to Japan twice. The first introduction was through the Buddhist discourses written in Chinese. The second and more recent introduction was through the Early Buddhist discourses written in the Pāli and Sanskrit languages. The Pāli discourses contained in the Tipiṭaka shocked Japanese scholars. Consequently, there are three technical terms for this important Buddhism: Primitive Buddhism, Fundamental Buddhism, or Early Buddhism.

Some Japanese scholars who were convinced of the superiority of Chinese Buddhism and Mahāyāna Buddhism insisted on calling Early Buddhism "Primitive Buddhism." This implies that Early Buddhism lacks proper structure.

On the other hand, the scholars and Buddhists who emphasize the fact that the Buddha's authentic voice is fundamental to all Buddhism, called it "Fundamental Buddhism," meaning that it is fundamental, basic, necessary, and of utmost importance.

Unlike either of these terms, Early Buddhism means the teaching of the Buddha from the early period. The technical term, Early Buddhism has neither the negative connotation of Primitive Buddhism nor the dogmatic meaning of Fundamental Buddhism.

Therefore, the Center for Early Buddhist Studies adopted the term Early Buddhism, which will be used whenever we discuss the authentic voice of the Buddha. This technical term follows today's trend in the world.

"Early Buddhism that contains the historical Sākyamuni Buddha's direct teaching is the Buddha's authentic voice and the root of Buddhism."

Why Early Buddhism?

We at the Center for Early Buddhist Studies made a vow to complete the translation of the Early Buddhist discourses, the Pāli Tipiṭaka. While translating the discourses we encountered this question many times, 'Why Early Buddhism?' The answer can be found in the following eight points:

1. Early Buddhism that recorded the Buddha's authentic voice is the starting point of Buddhism. As all trees have their roots, Buddhism's 2,600-year development has its roots in Early Buddhism. Just as trees cannot survive without roots, neither can Buddhism.

2. Early Buddhism is all Buddhism's standard and measuring stick. To know what Buddhism is and is not, one needs an objective standard. That standard cannot be anything but Early Buddhism. The core of Early Buddhism is the impermanence·suffering·non-self and Nibbāna. The impermanence·suffering·non-self are emphasized as the three characteristics [tilakkhana] in many places within the Early Buddhist discourses. Deliverance·Nibbāna are the ultimate happiness in Early Buddhism.

3. The teaching of Early Buddhism is based on rationalism and structuralism. It is analytical and has a direct correlation to modern methodology and quantitative science. Early Buddhism's theory and practice is organized into the five aggregates, the 12 sense bases, the 18 elements, the 22 faculties, the Four Noble Truths, the 12 links of dependent origination, and the 37 requisites of enlightenment. Early Buddhism provides scientific approaches to 'I' and 'the world.' Therefore, western Buddhists assert that Buddhism is a science.

4. Pāli and Sanskrit, the common languages used in the Early Buddhist discourses, have similar linguistic structures to the

Korean language. They use declensions in the same way as the Korean language. Therefore, because of similar grammar structure, chances of misinterpretation, distortion, and misunderstanding of the discourses by Korean scholars are considerably minimized.

5. The commentaries of the Early Buddhist discourses that contain interpretations still exist. These commentaries are the works of the Buddha's direct disciples such as the Venerable Sariputta.[4] Referencing these commentaries, Early Buddhism can avoid the risk of arbitrary interpretations and distortions of the Buddhist theory.

6. Buddhism started in the border region of modern day India and Nepal. The Buddha lectured in Pāli or in a language closest to Pāli. The Buddhist discourses of Mahāyāna Buddhism have been recorded in Sanskrit, a language closely related to Pāli. Therefore, to correctly understand and practice Buddhism, ultimately one must give serious consideration to the Pāli discourses. The Pāli Tipiṭaka has to be the primary Buddhist discourses.

7. By knowing the Buddha's authentic voice, one can look at Chinese Buddhism objectively. Through the knowledge of Early Buddhism, the Korean Buddhism that the Venerable Wonhyo and others of Korea have sought can be realized today.

8. Early Buddhism is the starting point for Korean Buddhism with its shrinking congregation. Early Buddhism [the roots] does not reject Mahāyāna Buddhism [the leaves]. When Mahāyāna Buddhism absorbs the nutritive elements of Early Buddhism and is saturated, the true Mahāyāna Buddhism – Korean Buddhism can flourish.

---

4 The Venerable Sariputta is one of the most important direct disciples of the Buddha.

"Early Buddhism, which recorded the Buddha's authentic voice, intact, is the starting point of Buddhism. As all trees have roots, Buddhism's 2,600-years of development has its roots in Early Buddhism."

The Purpose of Early Buddhism is the Realization of Happiness

Humans pursue happiness. Human activities – economic, political, cultural, philosophical, healing, and religious – are all in the pursuit of happiness. Such happiness is the fundamental purpose of Early Buddhism. In the Early Buddhist discourses, the Buddha defined happiness as the happiness of the present life, the happiness of the next life, and the ultimate happiness.

Humans desire to live happily by training for appropriate professional careers or trades, sharing their knowledge with society, and making a profit or earning wages. To cultivate a right human nature, one must live a morally wholesome life and help others. The Buddha called this morality [sīla] and generosity [dāna]. Likewise, one obtains happiness in the present life by learning and practicing one's appropriate skills, living a morally wholesome life, and helping others.

Religious activities are practiced by humans to gain happiness in the next life. The Buddha said the ways to be born as a human or in the celestial spheres would be through the practice of generosity and morality.

Generosity and morality were translated into Chinese as 施戒生天 [generosity-morality-birth in celestial spheres] and are familiar to Koreans. Generosity and morality are the first and second pāramitā[5] of six pāramitās of Mahāyāna Buddhism. The Buddha especially emphasized these two things to lay Buddhists. The Buddha said, "Help others, donate to the sangha, and live a morally wholesome life. Then one will be reborn in celestial spheres in the next life."

The third happiness the Buddha mentioned is the ultimate

---

5 Pāramitās mean perfection or the culmination of certain moralities.

happiness [parama-sukha], which means Nibbāna. Nibbāna is obtained through the practice [paṭi-padā] of the 37 requisites of enlightenment which culminates in the noble eightfold path. Buddhism's ultimate pursuit, realization, deliverance, Nibbāna, and attainment of Buddhahood are not found in any other value or faith systems in the world. This noble teaching is only offered in Buddhism. Bhikkhus[6] and bhikkhunis become monastics and practice to pursue this ultimate happiness. Buddhists seek happiness in the present and future lives through generosity and morality. Also, based on this foundation of generosity and morality, Buddhists cultivate greater insight [vipassanā] to realize the ultimate happiness of deliverance·Nibbāna. Indeed, the realization of Nibbāna is the happiness of all happinesses.

The venerable bhikkhus of China implicitly stated that the purpose of Buddhism is to eliminate suffering and obtain happiness. Happiness is not obtained by setting an ideal and pursuing it aimlessly. Rather, happiness is realized here, right now, when one eliminates suffering. Suffering and happiness are the two axes of the Four Noble Truths which define the eternal truth of Buddhism. They are the first truth [the noble truth of suffering] and the third truth [the noble truth of the cessation of suffering] of the Four Noble Truths.

Then, how does one eliminate suffering and gain happiness? Naturally one must eliminate the cause of suffering. The root of all suffering is craving [taṇhā]. When this cause is eliminated, suffering will be overcome. The elimination of craving is accomplished through practicing the noble eightfold path. Craving is the second truth [the noble truth of the origin of suffering]; practice is the fourth truth [the noble truth of the way leading to the cessation of suffering]. Thus, the purpose of Buddhism – 'to eliminate suffering and gain happiness' – is arranged beautifully as the Buddhism's truth, the Four Noble Truths.

---

6 A designation for Buddhist monk.

In many places within the Early Buddhist discourses, the Buddha's teaching is called Buddha-sāsana or Satthu-sāsana. Direct translations of these terms are the 'Buddha's command' or the 'Teacher's command.' The Buddha's command is for the happiness in the present life, the next life, and the realization of the ultimate happiness. However, no matter how noble the command is, unless one accurately comprehends command, one cannot follow it.

For the happiness of the present and next lives, we must live moral lives and help others. These are the commands of the Buddha found in the Early Buddhist discourses. This also is the true Mahāyāna Buddhism. For the ultimate happiness, one must have confidence in the Four Noble Truths and Nibbāna. This also is the Buddha's stern command. Just as there is no such thing as a vague command, there is no such thing as vague Buddhism. Only the student's ignorance makes the teacher's command seem vague.

"Buddhists pursue happiness.
The Buddha spoke of happiness in the present and next lives and the realization of the ultimate happiness.
Through acts of generosity and morality we can obtain happiness in the present and next lives.
The practice of Buddhism is the way to obtain the ultimate happiness."

The Basic Teaching of Early Buddhism

Early Buddhism's fundamental goal is Nibbāna, the realization of the ultimate happiness. Therefore, it is concluded that the "realization of Nibbāna [Nibbāna-sacchikiriyā] is the supreme happiness" in the Sutta-nipāta.[7] (Sn. 267) The realization of Nibbāna is the Buddha's stern command.

Then, how is Nibbāna realized? Naturally, Nibbāna is realized through the practice [paṭi-padā, bhāvanā]. In Early Buddhism, practicing means following the 37 requisites of enlightenment that are based on the noble eightfold path.

Can one realize Nibbāna if one practices the 37 requisites of enlightenment aimlessly? If one wants to practice the 37 requisites of enlightenment properly, one must have a correct understanding of 'I,' 'the world,' and 'the truth.' We call the Buddha's teaching about the correct understanding of the origin and cessation of suffering 'the theory [pariyatti].' Therefore, to realize Nibbāna one should not only understand the theory, but also put it into practice.

Suppose one can realize Nibbāna without understanding the theory and not putting it into practice. That would be like hoping to win the lottery.

Humans have three fundamental questions: 'What am I?' 'What is the world?' and 'What is the truth?' The Buddha, a teacher of humans and gods addressed these questions repeatedly. The Buddha considered the most important of these questions to be, 'What am I?' The Buddha's answer is, 'the five aggregates [pañca-kkhandha].' The 'I' is nothing but piles of the five aggregates: material form [rūpa][8], feeling [vedanā], perception [saññā],

---

7 The Sutta-nipāta [collection of discourses] is one of the earliest texts of the Pāli cannon and is the fifth book of the Khuddaka Nikāya.

8 Rūpa or form refers to material form [rūpa-khandha] of the five aggregates,

mental-formations [saṅkhārā], and consciousness [viññāṇa]. The Buddha's answer to, 'What is the world?' is, 'nothing but the 18 elements, which consist of the six internal sense bases [eye, ear, nose, tongue, body, and mind], the six external sense bases [visible form, sound, odor, taste, touch, and mental objects], and the six types of consciousness thereof.' Therefore, the five aggregates, the 12 sense bases, and the 18 elements are the basic principles behind all Buddhism.

'I' and 'the world' do not just exist by themselves. Furthermore, they are not created by the creator, the absolute being, gods or powerful beings. 'I' and 'the world' are dependently originated and are entanglements of various conditions that cause much suffering. The Buddha organized the origin and cessation of suffering in 'I' and 'the world' as the 12 links of dependent origination [paṭicca-samuppāda].

The Buddha named these truths the Four Noble Truths [cattari ariya-saccāni] through the insight of dependent origination of the suffering that exists here in 'I' and 'the world,' the origin of suffering, the cessation of suffering, and the way leading to the cessation of suffering.

When one practices the Dhamma of the 37 requisites of enlightenment with this understanding about 'I,' 'the world,' and 'the truth,' one realizes Nibbāna. The 37 requisites of enlightenment are the four foundations of mindfulness, the four right efforts, the four bases for spiritual power, the five faculties, the five powers, the seven factors of enlightenment, and the noble eightfold path.

Early Buddhism's theory and practice are organized as the five aggregates, the 12 sense bases, the 18 elements, the 22 faculties, the Four Noble Truths, the 12 links of dependent origination, and the 37 requisites of enlightenment. The 37 requisites of enlightenment

---

visible form [rūpa-āyatana] of the six external sense objects, or mind and body or name and form [nāma-rūpa] of the 12 links of dependent origination.

are the main topic of the fifth volume of the Saṁyutta Nikāya. The Path of Purification, the basis of Theravada Buddhism and the core of the commentaries explains the aggregates, the sense bases, the elements, the faculties, the truths, and dependent origination as being the soil of insight. (Vis.XIV.32) The *Prajñāpāramitā-Hṛdaya Discourse*[9] that Korean Buddhists chant morning and night also contains five of these basic theories: the aggregates, the sense bases, the elements, the truths, and dependent origination.

"Early Buddhism's basic teachings consist of both theory and practice. The theory includes the five aggregates, the 12 sense bases, the 18 elements, the 22 faculties, the Four Noble Truths, and the 12 links of dependent origination. The practice is explained by the 37 requisites of enlightenment, which is made up of the four foundations of mindfulness, the four right efforts, the four bases for spiritual power, the five faculties, the five powers, the seven factors of enlightenment, and the noble eightfold path."

---

9 The *Prajñāpāramitā-Hṛdaya Discourse*, also known as the Heart Sūtra, is a very well-known discourse of Mahāyāna Buddhism. It is short in comparison to other discourses and reciting this discourse at the morning and evening prayers is a well-established practice in Korea.

The Core of Early Buddhism is 'Dhamma'

The Buddha's teaching [sāsana] is called Buddhism or Dhamma. Thus, Buddhism, and especially Early Buddhism, is a construct with Dhamma as its core. Therefore, the word Buddha-Dhamma is very familiar to us. Let's look at the passages that emphasize Dhamma in the Early Buddhist discourses.

First, the fifth week after the Buddha attained enlightenment but prior to letting anyone know about it, he sat under the goat herder's banyan tree [nigrodha tree] on the bank of the Nerañjara River[10] in Uruvelā[11] and came to the following conclusion (AA.iii.24):

> "It is painful to dwell without reverence and deference. Now what samaṇa or brahmin can I honor, respect, and dwell in dependence on? . . . Let me then honor, respect, and dwell in dependence only on this Dhamma to which I have become fully enlightened." (A4:21, the Uruvela Discourse)

Second, the discourse that contains the Buddha's first teaching is called the *Setting in Motion the Wheel of Dhamma*. From this discourse the Buddha, centered on the noble eightfold path, proclaimed the middle path and the Four Noble Truths. Therefore, Dhamma which the Buddha had honored, respected, and dwelt in dependence on and to which he became fully enlightened are the Four Noble Truths [the theory] and the noble eightfold path [the practice].

Third, the Buddha told bhikkhus to, "Teach Dhamma," and requested that they transmit Dhamma as follows:

---

10 The Nerañjara river runs past Bodh Gayà, the place where the Buddha attained enlightenment.
11 Uruvelā is a small village near Bodh Gayà.

13

"Bhikkhus, I am freed from all snares, both celestial and human. You too, bhikkhus, are freed from all snares, both celestial and human. Wander forth, O bhikkhus, for the welfare of the multitude, for the happiness of the multitude, out of compassion for the world, for the good, welfare, and happiness of devas[12] and humans. Let not two go the same way. Teach, O bhikkhus, Dhamma that is good in the beginning, good in the middle, good in the end, with the right meaning and phrasing. Reveal the perfectly complete and purified holy life." (S4:5, the Māra's Snare Discourse 2) (Vin.i.20, the Great Chapter)

Fourth, the Buddha's respectful attitude toward Dhamma continued in his teaching: live "with Dhamma as an island, with Dhamma as your refuge." (D16)

Fifth, the Buddha sincerely asked bhikkhus in the *Dhammadāyāda Discourse*, "Bhikkhus, be my heirs in Dhamma, not my heirs in material things." (M3) Monastics must take this deep into their heart.

Sixth, in the *Vakkali Discourse*, the Buddha said to the Venerable Vakkali who was near death, "Enough, Vakkali! Why do you want to see this foul body? One who sees Dhamma sees me; one who sees me sees Dhamma. For in seeing Dhamma, Vakkali, one sees me; and in seeing me, one sees Dhamma." (S22:87) Afterward, the Buddha taught the impermanence·suffering·non-self of the five aggregates and the revulsion-dispassion-deliverance-knowledge of liberation.

Seventh, the teachings of the *Vakkali Discourse* are carried out in the *Vajracchedika Prajnaparamita Discourse* [the Diamond Sūtra], a long-held discourse of the Jogye Order of Korean Buddhism, with the following emphasis:

---

12 Here, devas refer to divine beings, gods, any superhuman being or beings regarded to be in certain respects above the human level.

"One who sees me as body or
follows me by voice,
will walk the wrong path and
will not see Tathāgata"[13]

In the *Diamond Sūtra*, the original texts in Sanskrit continue
as follows:

"One must see Buddhas as Dhamma
[dharmato Buddhā draṣṭavyā]
because Buddhas use Dhamma as their bodies.
[dharmakāyā hī nāyakāh]"

If one sees the Buddha as a body, then the Buddha also is
subject to death. As long as one sees the Buddha as a body, one
cannot escape the issue of life and death. The only way to solve
the issue of life and death is to see Dhamma and to realize Nibbāna, the unconditioned.[14]

Eighth, just before his passing, the Buddha left his first dying
instruction, "Dhamma and discipline will, at my passing, be your
teacher." (D16.6.1)

The Buddha wholeheartedly said the following:

"Ananda, it may be that you will think: 'The Teacher's instruction has ceased, now we have no teacher!' It should not be
seen like this, Ananda, for what I have taught and explained
to you as Dhamma and discipline will, at my passing, be your
teacher." (D16, the Mahaparinibbāna Discourse)

Ninth, the Venerable Ananda's conversations with the brahmin Gopaka Moggallāna clearly stated, "We are not without
a refuge, brahmin. We have a refuge; we have Dhamma as our
refuge." (M108)

---

13 Tathāgata is a Pāli word that the Buddha used when referring to himself.
14 Nibbāna is unconditioned reality.

Tenth, the Buddha left this dying instruction, "Dhamma and discipline will, at my passing, be your teacher." (D16. 6.1)

To honor the Buddha's dying instruction, the 500 Arahants chanted together Dhamma and compiled the *Collection of Discourses* at the First Buddhist Council, which was convened two months after the passing of the Buddha. At this Council, they also chanted together the rules of conduct and compiled the *Collection of Rules of Conduct.*

Right after the Buddha attained enlightenment, he said he would dwell in dependence only on Dhamma to which he had become fully enlightened. He emphasized Dhamma in his 45 years of teaching and he gave his dying instruction at the final passing [parinibbāna]: "Dhamma will be your teacher." Therefore, now, without the presence of the Buddha, what else can we Buddhists do but respect, learn, understand, and practice Dhamma?

"The Buddha's teaching is called Buddhism or Dhamma. Thus, Dhamma is the core of Early Buddhism."

What is Dhamma?

What is dhamma? How does one define dhamma? In the Early Buddhist discourses, dhamma has multiple meanings and can be classified largely into two categories. First, it can mean the Buddha's teaching. In this case, it is capitalized as Buddha-Dhamma. Second, it can mean all phenomena [sabbe-dhammā]. In this case, the lower case is used.

First, the Buddha's teaching, Dhamma, is organized into the theory and practice. The theory is categorized into six subjects – the five aggregates, the 12 sense bases, the 18 elements, the 22 faculties, the Four Noble Truths, and the 12 links of dependent origination. The practice is explained by the 37 requisites of enlightenment, which is categorized into seven subjects – the four foundations of mindfulness, the four right efforts, the four bases for spiritual power, the five faculties, the five powers, the seven factors of enlightenment, and the noble eightfold path. The theory and practice are further classified into the threefold training [morality, concentration, and wisdom] and Samatha-Vipassanā.

Second, after the passing [parinibbanā] of the Buddha, his direct disciples seriously analyzed, categorized, and systematized Dhamma, which is the foundation of the Abhidhamma. The literal meaning of the Abhidhamma is 'about Dhamma' or 'superior Dhamma.' The Abhidhamma is the systematic research of Dhamma, the core of the Buddha's teaching.

The dhamma, as in all phenomena [sabbe-dhamma], is the basic component that makes up all phenomena. In the Abhidhamma, it is defined as 'an ultimate component, with its own unique character, that cannot be deconstructed further.' (DhsA.39 Etc.) The dhamma as the smallest component is called the ultimate reality [paramattha dhamma]. In the Theravada Abhidhamma, all phenomena are categorized into one of four groups consisting of 82 unique dhammas. These four groups are consciousness [citta], mental factors [cetasikas], materiality [rūpa], and Nibbāna. In the Sabbatthivada [Sarvâstivāda] school of Indian Abhidhamma Buddhism, all phenomena are categorized into one of five groups consisting of 75 unique dhammas. These five groups are consciousness [citta], mental factors [cetasikas], materiality [rūpa], factors not directly associated with a specific mental function [citta-vippayutta-dhammā], and Nibbāna. In the Yogācāra school [the Consciousness-only school], all phenomena are categorized into one of five groups consisting of 100 unique dhammas.

All things composed of these smallest components are called concepts [paññatti]. For example, people, animals, mountains, rivers, computers, etc. are only concepts and do not belong to the domain of the dhamma, because they can be deconstructed into smaller components. A river is made up of water elements [āpo-dhātu] that flow and is only a concept that the mind created.

In the *Vajira Discourses*, it is said, "Just as, with an assemblage of parts, the word 'chariot' is used, so, when the aggregates exist, there is the convention 'a sentient being.'" (S5:10)

Here, the 'chariot' is an example of a concept and the 'parts' is an example of the dhamma. In Early Buddhism, the reason for seeing the concept of 'I' as the 'five aggregates' is to show clearly suffering and the non-self of the five aggregates. When one deconstructs and sees all conceptual entities as dhammas, the impermanence·suffering·non-self of these will be clearly seen. When one clearly sees the impermanence·suffering·non-self of these, one will experience revulsion, dispassion, and realize deliverance·Nibbāna. This is the consistent teaching of the early Buddhist discourses.

On the one hand, not only Theravada Buddhism but also all Northern Abhidharma Buddhism starting with Sarvâstivāda,[15] and Mahāyāna Buddhism starting with Mādhyamaka, selected

---

15 Sarvâstivāda is one of the major branches of Indian Abhidharma Buddhism.

specific characteristics [sabhāva-lakkhaṇa] and general characteristics [sāmañña-lakkhaṇa] as the way to contemplate dhammas. Early Buddhism's theory and practice system can be reduced to 'confirmation of general characteristics of specific characteristics.' Once dhammas are sorted by their specific characteristics, one can see clearly the general characteristics [impermanence·suffering·non-self] of the particular dhamma.

"Dhamma can mean the Buddha's teaching or the basic component which makes up all phenomena. The dhamma is the ultimate reality [paramattha dhamma]."

The Defining Characteristic of Early Buddhism is 'Seeing Deconstructively'

If one is asked to summarize Early Buddhism's definitive character in a few words, without hesitation, one can reply 'seeing deconstructively.' The term 'deconstruction' appeared in the Early Buddhist discourses. In the *Over a Thousand Discourse*, (S8:8) the Venerable Vangisa, who was admired as the most accomplished in inspiration among the Buddha's disciples and also was well versed in composing poems, praised the Buddha by saying, "He teaches . . . by deconstructing into parts." (S8:8) Here, deconstruction is translated from pavibhajja or vibhajja.

The technical term, vibhajja defines Theravada Buddhism, which preserved the Pāli Tipiṭaka intact for 2,600 years. They proudly called themselves vibhajja-vaadin [ones who teach deconstruction]. Japanese scholars translated this particular Theravada Buddhism as Discernment Theravada Buddhism. However, since the term 'discernment' can be considered somewhat disparaging, it is rarely used.

So, what is deconstructed? The concept [paññatti] is deconstructed into dhammas. The most important reasons for seeing deconstructively are as follows:

First, when one deconstructs and sees all conditioned phenomena as dhammas, one can eliminate the confusion and the fixed idea that the self, humans, sentient beings, the spirit, the universe, etc., are unchanging and permanent realities.

Second, these dhammas' momentary nature is seen only when all conditioned phenomena are deconstructed. By seeing clearly dhammas' momentary nature, the fact that all conditioned phenomena are suffering sinks deep into one's heart. Also the fact that all conditioned phenomena do not arise by themselves but are a dependently originated flow of phenomena becomes clearly visible.

When the conceptual entities such as the self, humans, and so forth are left bundled up, their impermanence·suffering·non-self cannot be clearly seen. Therefore, in the Abhidhamma, all conditioned phenomena are completely dismantled and deconstructed as dhammas before they are analyzed.

Seeing deconstructively, the conceptual being of 'I' is seen as the five aggregates, 'all beings' are seen as the 12 sense bases, 'the world' is seen as the 18 elements, 'the truths' are seen as the Four Noble Truths, and 'the life and death issue' is seen as the 12 links of dependent origination. Then all conditioned phenomena's [saṅkhara-dhammā] impermanent·suffering·non-self nature becomes clearly visible. After seeing clearly, the impermanence·suffering·non-self of all conditioned phenomena, one realizes the revulsion-dispassion-deliverance·Nibbāna. This teaching appears 450 times within the Early Buddhist discourses.

For example, no one thinks a fallen strand of hair on the ground is beautiful. We consider the hair beautiful and arouse a craving for it only when it is a specific color and style, and is bound to a woman's head. Our concept of beauty originates from our distorted notion of whole or partial images [like the face or head]. When one deconstructs and sees the hair as 'only hair,' it is no longer an object of craving, but rather an object of revulsion.

No matter how beautiful a woman's eyes, nose, and lips are, it is only so when these form whole or partial images. If eyes, nose, and lips are cut out and put in a jar of alcohol, no one would find them desirable! If they are seen deconstructively, the impermanence·suffering·non-self will be clearly seen, and revulsion will arise.

The core practice method of the Early Buddhist discourses such as the Dīgha Nikāya (D22) is seeing deconstructively. First, one deconstructs 'I' into body, feeling, mind, and mental objects. Then one concentrates [samatha] on one of these four objects and sees clearly with insight [vipassanā] the impermanence·suffering·non-self of the object. The word vipassanā means 'deconstruct [vi] and see [passanā].' If one cannot see deconstructively, one is not a Buddhist practitioner. If one cannot see 'I,' 'the self,' 'the world,' 'the truths,' and 'the life and death issue' deconstructively as the five aggregates, the 12 sense bases, the 18 elements, the 22 faculties, the Four Noble Truths, and the 12 links of dependent origination, one cannot realize enlightenment. One is deceived when phenomena are bundled up. One perceives the truth only when they are deconstructed. In Seon Buddhism of China, sharp insight [vipassanā], achieved through seeing deconstructively has been compared to a sword and is called Chuīmáo jiàn [吹毛劍]. It means a sharp edged sword [劍] that can cut a blowing [吹] hair [毛].

To see the world as emptiness [śūnyatā] is the intuitive view of Mādhyamaka. To see the world as magnificent beautiful flowers from the enlightened stance is the comprehensive view of the Hwaeom.[16] Alternatively, Early Buddhism realizes enlightenment by deconstructing and seeing the world as dhammas. Even if one does not see deconstructively but sees rather with intuition 'I' and 'the world' as emptiness, ultimately deconstruction must be applied to reveal emptiness.

Therefore, whether one emphasizes the deconstructive view of Abhidhamma [Abhidharma] and Yogācāra, emphasizes the intuitive view of Mādhyamaka, or emphasizes the comprehensive view of Hwaeom, all methods must be based on deconstruction, the methodology of Buddhism. It would not be too late to practice the intuitive and comprehensive views after strengthening the foundation of deconstruction. I maintain that Early Buddhism's emphasis on deconstruction is truly needed in today's Korean Buddhism, which currently only emphasizes the intuitive and comprehensive views.

---

16 Hwaeom is the name of the Korean transmission of the Huayan school of Chinese Buddhism.

"The hallmark of Early Buddhism is seeing deconstructively.
What is deconstructed?
The concept is deconstructed into the dhamma.
Without seeing the concept, deconstructively,
deliverance·Nibbāna cannot be realized.
One is deceived by the bundled-up concept
but realizes the truth when it is deconstructed."

The Theory of Early Buddhism

❧ CHAPTER 2

What Am I?

The Five Aggregates:
I Am the Five Aggregates

On the terrace of the palace, King Pasenadi and Queen Mallika of Kosala exchanged the following conversations in the *Mallika Discourse:*

> "Is there, Mallika, anyone more dear to you than yourself?"
> "There is no one, great king, more dear to me than myself. But is there anyone, great king, more dear to you than yourself?"

> "For me too, Mallika, there is no one more dear than myself."

The King approached the Blessed One and related this conversation. Then the Blessed One recited the following verse:

> "Having traversed all quarters with the mind, one finds none anywhere dearer than oneself. Likewise, each person holds himself most dear; Hence one who loves himself should not harm others." (S3:8, the Mallika Discourse)

This well-known verse appears in the *Udana Discourse* of the Khuddaka Nikāya (Ud.47) and the Path of Purification (Vis.IX.10). So, what is 'I,' the most important subject to all people? 'What am I?' is the most frequently asked question of oneself from the beginning of humanity. Naturally, since it is a very important question, the Buddha answered this question repeatedly. How did the Buddha answer this question?

The Buddha said many times, simply and plainly, in the Early Buddhist discourses that "'I' is the five aggregates." The 'I' is material form, feeling, perception, mental formations, and consciousness – a pile of the five aggregates.

First, in the discourses, material form [rūpa] is defined: "It is deformed, therefore it is called [material] form." (S22:79) Here, deformation does not mean change. Deformation means that material form's shape can alter. This is a characteristic of material form. Feeling, perception, mental formations, and consciousness can change but cannot deform, because they have neither form nor shape. Deformation is a unique character of material form.

Second, feeling [vedanā] is what triggers the first spark of emotional, sentimental, and artistic mental formations. For example, desire and anger are mental formations based on feeling but do not belong to the area of feeling.

These belong to the fourth of the five aggregates, mental formations. Therefore, feeling is the first trigger of emotional and sentimental mental formations. According to the discourses, there are three kinds of feelings: pleasant feeling, painful feeling, and neutral feeling.

Third, perception [sañña] is what triggers intellectual, conceptual, and philosophical mental formations. Mental formations such as delusion, insight, and wrong view are based on perception but do not belong to the area of perception. These belong to the fourth of the five aggregates, mental formations. Therefore, perception is the first trigger of intellectual and philosophical mental formations. It is possible for perception to change quickly. It is related to the identity view [sakkāya-ditthi]. Inversions of perception concerning permanence, pleasure, self, and attractiveness result in the development of delusion.

Fourth, mental formations [saṅkhāra] are psychological phenomena. The mental formations of the five aggregates always appear in a plural form. The consistent explanations within the commentaries, the sub-commentaries, and the Abhidhamma are that mental formations contain 50 mental factors – all 52 mental factors [cetasika] except feeling and perception.

Fifth, consciousness [viññāna] allows one to know an object with the help of feeling, perception, and mental formations. In many Early Buddhist discourses, it is stated, "It cognizes, therefore it is called consciousness." (S22:79) The Early Buddhist discourses, the Abhidhamma, and the Yogācāra discourses explain that mind [citta], mind [mano], and consciousness [viññāna] all have the same meaning.

Why did the Buddha say that the being, 'I,' is the five aggregates? Because this says clearly that there exists no permanent essence [sāra] of 'I' or self.

Therefore, Bhikkhuni Vajira[1] recited the following:

"Just as, with an assemblage of parts,
The word 'chariot' is used,
So, when the aggregates exist,
There is the convention 'a sentient being.'"
(S5:10, the Vajira Discourse)

By seeing the being, 'I' deconstructively as body, feeling, perception, mental formations, and consciousness, impermanent and momentary character or impermanence of the five aggregates is clearly seen. The impermanent and changing nature of phenomena is suffering. We don't refer to the impermanent and suf-

---

1 Bhikkhuni Vajira is a Buddhist nun mentioned in the Early Buddhist discourses.

fering phenomena as 'I' or 'myself.' When we see impermanence with insight, we can clearly see suffering and non-self. When we thoroughly observe the impermanence·suffering·non-self, the seemingly impossible deliverance of sentient beings can finally be accomplished.

"The Buddha said, simply and plainly, in many places within the Early Buddhist discourses, 'I' is the five aggregates. It means, the being, 'I,' is nothing but material form, feeling, perception, mental formations, and consciousness – only a pile of the five aggregates."

The Five Aggregates: Material Form

In the Early Buddhist discourses, material form is explained, "Bhikkhus, the four great elements and the [material] form derived from the four great elements: this is called [material] form." (S12:2, the Analysis of Dependent Origination Discourse)

The Venerable Sariputta said, "And what is the material form aggregate affected by clinging? It is the four great elements and the material form derived from the four great elements. And what are the four great elements? They are the earth element, the water element, the fire element, and the air element." (M28, the Greater Discourse on the Simile of the Elephant's Footprint Discourse) As such, he explained two types of material form: basic elements and derived elements. The basic elements are the four great elements [earth, water, fire, and air]. There are 24 elements derived from the basic elements.

Thus, Theravada Buddhism recognizes 28 elements in all – the four great elements [the basic elements: earth, water, fire, and air] and the 24 derived elements. These are classified further into 18 produced and ten unproduced materialities.

The 18 produced materialities are the four great elements [earth, water, fire, and air], the five physical sense organs [eye, ear, nose, tongue, and body], the four objective material phenomena [visible form, sound, odor, and taste], the two sexual phenomena [femininity and masculinity], the heart phenomenon [heart base], the life phenomenon [life faculty], and the nutritional phenomenon [nutriment]. These materialities' characters are called the unproduced materialities. There are ten kinds of unproduced materialities. They are classified in the area of materiality [space element, bodily intimation, vocal intimation, lightness, malleability, and wieldiness] plus the four specific characteristics of materialities [production, continuity, decay, and impermanence].

The four great elements or the basic elements are not the literal real earth, water, fire, and air but rather mean the earth element [pathavī-dhātu], the water element [āpo-dhātu], the fire element [tejo-dhātu], and the air element [vāyo-dhātu].

The earth elements are hardness and softness, roughness and smoothness, and heaviness and lightness; the water elements are fluidity and cohesion; the fire elements are heat and cold; and the air elements are distention and motion. The four great elements are the fundamental elements that constitute material form or materiality. They cannot be separated and are compounded into all material of various forms. In the Abhidhamma, materiality is produced by four causes [consciousness, kamma, temperature, and nutriment]. Every moment the consciousness of the specific instant arises, stays, and perishes; the resulting materiality is produced in each instant by that specific consciousness and prior kamma.

A pile of material form is defined in the Early Buddhist discourses: "It is deformed, bhikkhus, therefore it is called [material] form. Deformed by what? Deformed by cold, deformed by heat, deformed by hunger, deformed by thirst, deformed by contact with flies, mosquitoes, wind, sun, and serpents." (S22:79, the Being Devoured Discourse)

Here, deformation [ruppana] is different from change [viparinnama]. Deformation means that material form's shape can alter. This is a characteristic of material form.

Why did the Buddha define material form or body as deformed? Because when my body is seen deconstructively deformation or impermanence is clearly seen. By seeing impermanence of material form, defined as deformation, we realize liberation.

"It is deformed, therefore it is called material form. Deformation means that material form's shape can alter. This is a characteristic of material form. By seeing impermanence of material form, defined as deformation, we realize liberation."

The Five Aggregates: Feeling

For the question of 'What am I?' the Buddha's second answer is feeling [vedanā]. Feeling is the most sensitive subject in a capitalist society. Among the five aggregates, only feeling is treated as an independent subject in the Saṁyutta Nikāya. The *Vedanāsaṁyutta* (S36) of the Saṁyutta Nikāya contains 31 discourses. The following are a few perspectives on feeling:

First, feeling is the first trigger of the emotional, sentimental, and artistic mental formations.

Second, according to the discourses, there are three modes of feeling – pleasant, painful, and neutral.

> "And why, bhikkhus, do you call it feeling? 'It feels,' bhikkhus, therefore it is called feeling. And what does it feel? It feels pleasure, it feels pain, it feels neither-pain-nor-pleasure. 'It feels,' therefore it is called feeling." (S22:79, the Being Devoured Discourse)

Third, these three feelings [pleasant, painful, and neutral] are connected to the latent propensity of lust, hatred, and delusion, respectively.

> "Bhikkhus, the underlying tendency to lust should be abandoned in regard to pleasant feeling. The underlying tendency to hatred should be abandoned in regard to painful feeling. The underlying tendency to delusion should be abandoned in regard to neutral feeling." (S36:3, the Abandonment Discourses)

Fourth, perception is deeply connected to a socialist society that values ideology. Feeling is deeply connected to the development of capitalism and is connected to emotion, sentiment, art, and pursuit of convenience.

Fifth, feeling inevitably arises. There is no way to avoid it. The Buddha said, "They converge upon feeling." (A8:83, the Rooted Discourse)

According to the Southern Abhidhamma, the Northern Abhidharma, and the Yogācāra discourses, feeling is included in the seven universal mental factors [contact, feeling, perception, volition, one-pointedness, life faculty, and attention] that arise with consciousness. Therefore, as long as one exists, one cannot escape from feeling unless one is in the state of 'cessation of feeling and perception [saññā-vedayita-nirodha]' or 'attainment of extinction [nirodha-samāpatti].'

Sixth, because feeling is unavoidable, the Buddha emphasized practicing concentration to increase the purification, stability, and happiness of feeling. Likewise, the four jhānas and the nine graduated concentrations [the four jhānas, the four formless concentrations, and the state of cessation of feeling and perception] are emphasized.

Seventh, the Buddha earnestly said not to get struck with a 'second dart:'

> "Bhikkhus, suppose they were to strike a man with a dart, but they would not strike him immediately afterwards with a second dart, so that the man would feel a feeling caused by one dart only. So too, when the instructed noble disciple is contacted by a painful feeling, he doesn't sorrow, grieve, and lament; he doesn't weep beating his breast and become distraught. He feels one feeling, a bodily one, not a mental one." (S36:6, the Dart Discourse)

Eighth, then how does one cope with the unavoidable painful feeling?

> "Bhikkhus, while a bhikkhu dwells thus, mindful and clearly comprehending, diligent, ardent, and resolute, if there arises in him a painful feeling, he understands thus: 'There has arisen

in me a painful feeling. Now that is dependent, not independent. Dependent on what? Dependent on just this body. But this body is impermanent, conditioned, dependently arisen. So when the painful feeling has arisen in dependence on a body that is impermanent, conditioned, dependently arisen, how could it be permanent?' He dwells contemplating impermanence in the body and in painful feeling, he dwells contemplating vanishing, contemplating fading away, contemplating cessation, contemplating relinquishment. As he dwells thus, the underlying tendency to hatred in regard to the body and in regard to painful feeling is abandoned by him." (S36:7, the Sick Ward Discourse)

The Buddha explained pleasant and calm feelings with the same method.

Ninth, however, the Buddha concluded that, "feeling is like a water bubble." (S22:95, the Lump of Foam Discourse) Thus, it is explained in the commentaries that as a bubble arises on the surface of water and does not last for long, so too with feeling, for it is said that 100,000 kotis[2] of sensory impulses arise and cease in the body in the time of a finger snap. Therefore, don't get attached to these feelings, but rather understand their impermanent nature. One must accomplish the revulsion-dispassion-deliverance-knowledge of liberation by seeing clearly the impermanence-suffering-non-self of feeling. In many places within the Early Buddhist discourses, one is instructed to realize the 'happiness of Nibbāna' and not the 'feeling of happiness.'

"Feeling is like a water bubble.
Don't get attached to these feelings.
One must deeply reflect on the impermanence of feelings."

---

2 One koti equals 10 million.

The Five Aggregates:
Perception

The Buddha's third answer to the question of 'What am I?' is perception [sañña]. Examination of perception from several perspectives reveals the following:

First, if feeling, the second factor of the five aggregates is the first trigger of emotional, sentimental, and artistic mental formations, then perception is the basis for intellectual ideological, and philosophical mental formations.

Second, if feeling, which is connected to emotion, sentiment, art, and the pursuit of convenience is closely tied to the development of capitalism, perception is more closely tied to socialism, which values ideology.

Third, according to the Southern Abhidhamma, the Northern Abhidharma, and the Yogācāra discourses, perception belongs to mental formations that arise with consciousness – the seven universal mental factors [contact, feeling, perception, volition, one-pointedness, life faculty, and attention]. Therefore, as long as a sentient being exists, and unless that being is in the state of 'cessation of feeling and perception' or 'attainment of extinction,' one cannot escape from perception. Because one cannot escape from perception, the Buddha strongly indicated which perceptions to keep and which perceptions to abandon.

Fourth, one must abandon unwholesome perceptions. Perception's function is to recognize, identify objects, and arouse concepts. By the way, in the Early Buddhist discourses, perception is mentioned as being unwholesome and it needs to be overcome because these conceptualizations arouse myriads of clinging and unwholesome mental formations. Therefore, one is instructed not to delight in and enjoy "mental proliferations [papañca-sañña]." (M1; M18)

The *Diamond Sūtra* [the Vajracchedikā Prajñāpāramitā Sūtra], instructs us of those unwholesome perceptions about self, individuals, sentient beings, and soul which we should abandon. Bhikkhu Kumārajīva[3] understood that these perceptions do not only stay as perceptions but also adhere to ontological fixed ideas. He translated perception as a notion [相] and not as perception [想] in the *Diamond Sūtra*. Five of the six bhikkhus [all except for Bhikkhu Kumārajīva], who translated the discourses from Indian to Chinese, used 'perception' as a literal translation of 想.

Fifth, there are the inversions of perception. This is when one considers impermanent, suffering, non-self, and unattractive to be permanent, pleasurable, self, and attractive. (A4:49) The *Heart Sūtra* [the Mahā-Prajñāpāramitā-Hṛdaya-Sūtra] emphasizes that one must abandon these inversions and focus on realizing the ultimate happiness, Nibbāna. These inversions of perception are described in the Nikāya as follows:

"Bhikkhus, there are these four inversions of perception, inversions of mind, and inversions of view. What four? 1) The inversion of perception, mind, and view that takes the impermanent to be permanent; 2) the inversion of perception, mind, and view that takes what is suffering to be pleasurable; 3) the inversion of perception, mind, and view that takes what is non-self to be self; 4) the inversion of perception, mind, and view that takes what is unattractive to be attractive. These are the four inversions of perception, mind, and view." (A4:49, the Inversions Discourse)

"The inversions are the three, namely, inversion of perception, of mind, and of view, which occur apprehending objects that

---

3 Bhikkhu Kumārajīva [344–413 CE] is well known for prolific translations of the Buddhist discourses from Sanskrit to Chinese.

are impermanent, suffering, non-self, and unattractive, as permanent, pleasurable, self, and attractive." (Vis.XXII.53)

Sixth, since perception always arises with consciousness, ontological perception that obstructs deliverance·Nibbāna must be abandoned and perception that helps deliverance·Nibbāna must be developed.

Therefore, in the Early Buddhist discourses, there are lists that contain both perceptions of fixed ideas which should be discarded and perceptions that should be developed and practiced for liberation and the realization of deliverance·Nibbāna. In the Aṅguttara Nikāya there are lists that contain various combinations of perceptions for practitioners.

For example, the *Book of the Tens* in the Aṅguttara Nikāya lists, "1) The perception of impermanence, 2) the perception of non-self, 3) the perception of unattractiveness, 4) the perception of danger, 5) the perception of abandoning, 6) the perception of dispassion, 7) the perception of cessation, 8) the perception of non-delight in the entire world, 9) the perception of impermanence in all conditioned phenomena, and 10) mindfulness breathing." (A10:60, the Girimānanda Discourse)

Various combinations of perceptions related to the practice appear in the Early Buddhist discourses. These perceptions must be obtained through the practice. These perceptions are recommended as they are helpful to the realization of deliverance· Nibbāna.

Seventh, perception is compared to an incorporeal shimmering mirage in the Early Buddhist discourses. (S22:95) Therefore, we need to discard the unwholesome perceptions and fixed ideas like ego, the great self, the true self, soul, and one mind. We need to accomplish the revulsion-dispassion-deliverance with a deep understanding that these perceptions are truly "void, hollow, and insubstantial" (S22:95) and ultimately are impermanent· suffering·non-self. The Buddha's true student practices by walking the path of deliverance·Nibbāna.

"Perception's function is to recognize objects, identify objects, and arouse concepts. Conceptualizations arouse myriads of clinging and unwholesome mental formations."

The Five Aggregates:
Mental Formations

The Buddha's fourth answer to 'What am I?' is mental formations [saṅkhārā]. Here, the unfamiliar Pāli term saṅkhārā means 'mental formations' and is translated in Chinese as 'doing or conduct' [行]. Saṅkhārā is one of the most frequently used terms in the Early Buddhist discourses and can mean one of the following four things:

First, in the context of impermanence, it means all 'conditioned phenomena [saṅkhata-dhamma]' and not Nibbāna, which is unconditioned.

Second, in the Abhidhamma, when saṅkhārā appears as the fourth of the five aggregates it means mental formations. Remember, mental formations contain 50 mental factors – all 52 mental factors [cetasikā dhamma] except feeling and perception.

Third, when saṅkhārā appears as the second link of the 12 links of dependent origination, it is interpreted as volitional formations. In this case, saṅkhārā is synonymous with kamma.

Fourth, when saṅkhārā appears as bodily formations [kāya-saṅkhārā], verbal formations [vacī-saṅkhārā], and mental formations [mano-saṅkhārā] it is the same as the volitional formations of the 12 links of dependent origination, in other words, kamma formations. Also, depending on the context, it can mean a simple 'activity.' (S41:6)

Occasionally, some misunderstand and translate the mental formations of the five aggregates as volitional formations or kamma formations; this would be an incorrect translation because it only highlights intention [cetanā], which is a portion of the mental formations.

Examination of mental formations from several perspectives reveals the following:

First, the second factor of the five aggregates, feeling, is the first trigger of emotional, sentimental, and artistic mental formations. The third factor, perception, is the first trigger of intellectual, ideological, and philosophical mental formations. It must be noted that because mental formations include many mental factors with distinctive, separate, and unique characters, the term always appears in the plural form. The four remaining aggregates [material form, feeling, perception, and consciousness] appear in the singular form.

Second, there are 52 mental factors in total in the Theravada Abhidhamma. Excluding feeling and perception, the remaining 50 mental factors are the mental formations of the five aggregates.

The 52 mental factors are as follows:

- The 13 mental factors that become common with others: contact, feeling, perception, volition, one-pointedness, life faculty, attention, applied thought, sustained thought, determination, energy, rapture, and desire.
- The 14 unwholesome mental factors: delusion, shamelessness, disregard for consequence, restlessness, greed, wrong view, conceit, hatred, envy, miserliness, remorse, sloth, torpor, and doubt.
- The 25 beautiful mental factors: faith, mindfulness, moral shame, regard for consequence, non-greed, non-hatred, equanimity, tranquility of mental factors, tranquility of consciousness, lightness of mental factors, lightness of consciousness, pliancy of mental factors, pliancy of consciousness, wieldiness of mentor factors, wieldiness of consciousness, proficiency of mental factors, proficiency of consciousness, rectitude of mental factors, rectitude of consciousness, right speech, right action, right livelihood, compassion, sympathetic joy, and faculty of wisdom.

In the *Abhidharma-Kośa-Bhāsya* [the Commentary on the *Treasury of Abhidharma*][4] of the Northern Abhidharma, 46 mental formations are listed; in the Yogācāra discourses, 50 mental formations are listed. These mental formations arise and perish together with consciousness in groups according to various circumstances.

Third, these mental formations are compared to a plantain tree in the Early Buddhist discourses. (S22:95) It is stated in the commentaries, "As a plantain trunk is an assemblage of many sheathes, each with its own characteristic, so the clinging aggregate of mental formations is an assemblage of many mental factors, each with its own characteristic and function." (SA.ii.323)

Although the outward appearance of a plantain's trunk resembles a sturdy cement column, its core is hollow. Likewise, when our various and intense mental formations are bundled up, it looks as if it is solid. However, when it is dismantled and deconstructed with an 'ax of insight,' it is the same as the insubstantial plantain with a hollow core.

Therefore, this discourse concludes, "a bhikkhu inspects them, ponders them, and carefully investigates them. As he investigates them, they appear to him to be void, hollow, insubstantial. For what substance could there be in mental formations?" (S22:95, A Lump of Foam Discourse)

Fourth, the practitioner must use an 'ax of insight' to dismantle and deconstruct the mental formations that constitute 'I,' so that one can see clearly. One must deeply understand the insubstantial [asāra] nature of mental formations [in other words, non-self], then achieve realization through experiencing the revulsion-dispassion-deliverance-Nibbāna. One is deceived when mental formations are lumped together but achieves realization when they are deconstructed.

---

4 The Abhidharma-Kośa-Bhāsya is the commentary on the Abhidharma-Kośa [the Treasury of Abhidharma] written by Bhikkhu Vasubandhu.

"The mental formations are all except two [feeling and perception] of the 52 mental factors. These mental formations arise and perish together with consciousness in groups according to various circumstances."

The Five Aggregates: Consciousness

The Buddha's last answer to 'What am I?' is consciousness [viññāṇa]. In Korean, this is translated as consciousness [알음 알이]] and in Chinese as knowing [識]. Viññāṇa is a word derived from 'knowing deconstructively.' Examination of consciousness from several perspectives reveals the following:

First, from the Early Buddhist discourses to the Abhidharma and the Yogācāra discourses, mind [citta], mind [mano], and consciousness [viññāṇa] are synonyms. They are used differently depending on their context.

Second, in the Early Buddhist discourses, the mind only knows an object. The mind always arises and perishes with feeling, perception, and mental formations. The mind knows an object with the help of feeling, perception, and mental formations. The Abhidharma and the Yogācāra discourses agree on this point.

Third, the mind or consciousness dependently arises. Without a sense base and an object, consciousness cannot exist on its own or arise independently. Therefore, statements such as this appear in various places in the Early Buddhist discourses: "In dependence on the eye and [visible] forms, eye-consciousness arises." (S35:60)

Fourth, the mind arises and passes away moment-to-moment. The Buddha emphasized, "Bhikkhus, I do not see even one other thing that changes so quickly as the mind. It is not easy to give a simile for how quickly the mind changes." (A1:5:8) This teaching is called a 'moment' [khaṇa] in the commentaries and the Abhidharma. Furthermore, it is explained in the commentaries that this moment is made up of three sub-moments: arising, static, and passing away. So, even the slightest chance of falling into the substantiality of a moment is rejected.

Fifth, the mind is the continuity [santati] of consciousness.

If the mind arises and passes away moment-to-moment, then what is this mind that is here, now, and so vivid? Early Buddhism explains that the mind that is here, now, and vividly unfolding is the 'continuity of momentary arising and momentary passing away of consciousness.' This was emphasized in the commentaries as the undercurrent of life-continuum consciousness [bhavaṅga-sota]. (DA.ii.253) This continuity of consciousness appears as citta-dhāra in the *Diamond Sūtra*. Bhikkhu Hiuen Tsiang translated citta-dhāra as a continuous flow of consciousness [心流注].

Sixth, consciousness or the mind is impermanent. It has no substance. The impermanence of the five aggregates is explained in many places in the Early Buddhist discourses. The revulsion-dispassion-deliverance-knowledge of liberation are aroused when one deeply understands the impermanence·suffering·nonself. Only then can one accomplish liberation, realize Nibbāna, and become an Arahant. On the other hand, when the mind is 'absolutized,'[5] it has become 'the self' of the wrong path. If the five aggregates are absolutized, one thinks that a self exists. This is one aspect of the identity view. The identity view is the first of the ten fetters [saṃyojana] that shackles sentient beings as sentient beings. It is one of the four notions of a self, a person, a sentient being, and a life-span of the *Diamond Sūtra*. As long as one has the identity view, one cannot achieve even the first stage of attainment, the stream-enterer.

Lastly, I would like to emphasize that the mind is only one of the five aggregates. The mind should not be considered a creator or absolutized. Occasionally, some would absolutize the impermanent mind and say: 'Obtain Buddhahood through the realization of the mind,' 'the mind is the Buddha,' or 'all phenomena are created by the mind.' This puts the mind above a

---

5 Absolutized means declared complete or unchangeable.

monotheistic god. Of course, it does not appear to be problematic if one accepts this teaching to emphasize the fact that a creator or an absolute being does not exist, anywhere outside of the self. But if one believes in the absolutized mind, as if the mind is the creator or the absolute being who creates all phenomena in the universe, this is a huge problem!

The mind should never be absolutized. When the mind is absolutized, one falls immediately into the wrong path of the identity view. The teaching to absolutize and substantiate the mind does not appear anywhere in the Early Buddhist discourses. Instead, it is emphasized in various places in the Early Buddhist discourses that one must know that the mind is without substance, and to realize the ultimate happiness, Nibbāna.

I boldly propose that Korean Buddhism stops clinging to absolutization or substantiation of the mind. Instead, Korean Buddhists need to understand that the mind has no substance and realize the happiness of Nibbāna as shown by the Buddha.

"The mind is only one of the five aggregates. One should never absolutize the mind. If the mind is absolutized, one falls into the view that a self exists – in other words, the identity view."

The Five Aggregates:
The Five Aggregates do not Arise in Succession

Previously, the five piles of material form, feeling, perception, mental formations, and consciousness have been examined individually. A comprehensive review of the characteristics of the five aggregates shows the following:

First, the five aggregates do not arise in succession. Just because the five aggregates are examined individually, in order, it does not mean the five aggregates arise in succession. The five aggregates arise simultaneously. Surprisingly, there are many among Buddhists who insist the five aggregates arise in succession and give nonsensical explanations about this. One example of such nonsensical explanations would be, "One comes in contact with an object, then perceives or thinks about the object. Based on that perception, intentional actions arise which are then saved in the consciousness."

Clearly, the five aggregates never arise in succession. Instead, they arise simultaneously. The five aggregates arise and perish together moment-to-moment; this is common knowledge in the Southern Abhidhamma, the Northern Abhidharma, and the Yogācāra discourses which is the Mahāyāna Abhidharma.

Of course, at a specific moment, a specific one or more of the five aggregates can seem more intense. For example, when one sees a flower, feeling would be stronger; when one perceives and identifies an object, perception would be stronger; when one's desire to obtain arises, mental formations called lust would be stronger.

The Abhidhamma and the Yogācāra discourses clearly explain that feeling, perception, and mental formations are mental factors. These mental factors belong to the mind and arise and perish with the mind. Because they arise and perish together with the mind, they are called mental factors. When the five aggregates, the most important Dhamma of Buddhism, are considered to arise in succession, Buddhism becomes very confusing in my opinion.

Second, a true self does not exist. The five aggregates are the Buddha's answers to 'What am I?' No matter how hard one tries to find the everlasting and non-changing 'I,' one will not find 'I.' Buddhists must be able to answer, 'What am I?' without hesitation. They must answer 'I' am 'the five aggregates.' They must deconstruct and see 'I' as the five aggregates.

In all schools of Buddhism, the aggregates have no substance. When 'I' is deconstructed and seen as the five aggregates, the impermanence·suffering·non-self of 'I' is clearly evident. A deep understanding of this leads to the revulsion-dispassion-deliverance-knowledge of liberation and realization of Nibbāna. This is emphasized by the Buddha in many places in the Early Buddhist discourses.

Third, when 'I' is seen deconstructively as the five aggregates, the being of 'I' is nothing but a concept. This sort of conceptual entity does not have substance and is called paññatti. All that we know through names – humans, men, women, selves, sentient beings, souls, cars, computers, mountains, and rivers – are only conceptual phenomena. In Early Buddhism, the reason for seeing these conceptual phenomena after deconstructing them into the dhamma is to unveil clearly the impermanence·suffering·non-self of the dhammas.

No conditioned phenomena can escape from the general characteristics, the impermanence·suffering·non-self. Even a moment [the smallest unit] shows the unique character of the dhamma, a composition of three parts [arising, static, and passing away]. Therefore, a moment is nothing but a continuous flow. Accordingly, Early Buddhism does not insist on the existence of objective phenomena, but logically shows the emptiness of objective phenomena.

Early Buddhism and the Abhidhamma clearly explain the

non-self of all conditioned phenomena by deconstruction and analysis. It is difficult to show the non-self of all conditioned phenomena using intuition only. I think the intuitive approach of Mādhyamaka[6] would be clearer if it were based on analysis. Ultimately, the method based on deconstruction and analysis would result in intuition. It is not possible to realize the revulsion-dispassion-deliverance-knowledge of liberation only by analysis of the impermanence·suffering·non-self. Insight and intuition are both needed. The true middle path is possible when analysis and intuition support and restrain each other.

"No matter how earnestly one searches for the everlasting and non-changing 'I,' it is not obtainable. Buddhists' answer to the question 'What am I?' must be, without hesitation, 'the five aggregates.'"

---

6 The Mādhyamaka school of Buddhism is one of the two main schools of Mahāyāna Buddhism.

᭡ CHAPTER 3
What is the World?

The 12 Sense Bases

The most fundamental questions of human beings are, 'What am I?' and 'What is the world?' The Buddha, a great teacher of the three spheres[1] clearly answered these two questions. The answer to 'What am I?' is 'I am the five aggregates.' The answer to the questions, 'What is the world? What is a sentient being? What are all conditioned phenomena?' is 'the 12 sense bases [āyatana].' Therefore, the five aggregates encompass the Buddhism's view of humanity. The 12 sense bases define Buddhism's view of the world.

In the Early Buddhist discourses (S35:23, the All Discourse), it is explained that all conditioned phenomena are perceived through the 12 sense bases. No phenomena exist unless perceived through the 12 sense bases. In the *World Discourse* (S35:82) and other discourses, it is explained that we perceive 'the world' through these 12 sense bases. Besides the 12 sense bases, everything else is just a conceptual entity. Here the internal six sense

---

1 In Buddhist cosmology, the three spheres are the sensual-desire sphere, the form sphere, and the formless sphere.

bases or sense organs are eye, ear, nose, tongue, body, and mind [mano]; the external six sense bases or sense objects are visible forms, sound, odor, taste, tactile objects, and mental objects. According to the *Six Sense Bases Discourse* of the Saṁyutta Nikāya, the 12 sense bases, the six sense bases, the six internal and external sense bases are synonymous with one another, all with same content. (S35)

The Pāli words, dvadasa āyatana, translated as 'the 12 sense bases' is a combination of two words, dvadasa [12] and āyatana [place]. Āyatana is a word which frequently appears in the Brāhmana[2] of India's Brahmanism which preceded Buddhism. It means a place for religious service or a habitat for animals. According to the Path of Purification, āyatana has five meanings: "Base, [āyatana] should be understood in the sense of place of abode, store [mine], meeting place, locality of birth, and cause." (Vis.XV.5–7)

In Chinese, āyatana is translated as 'enter' [入] giving the importance to the literal meaning of 'coming this way.' It was also translated as 'place' [處] since it is used for a place. For example, the fifth of the 12 links of dependent origination is translated as six sense bases [六入]. The 12 sense bases [eye, visible form, and so forth] and the four formless attainments from the base of boundless space to the base of neither perception nor non-perception are translated as place [處].

The Buddha emphasized through the teaching of the 12 sense bases that the world or all conditioned phenomena cannot exist without the contact of internal and external sense bases [eye and visible form, ear and sound, nose and odor, tongue and taste, body and tactile object, and mind and mental object]. He is saying

---

2 The Brāhmana is a collection of ancient Indian texts with commentaries on the hymns of the four Vedas. They are primarily a digest incorporating myths, legends, explanation of Vedic rituals and in some cases philosophy.

that the world, beings, and all conditioned phenomena have no meaning apart from 'my issues' or 'my circumstances.'

Thus, by deconstructing and seeing conceptual entities like the world or all conditioned phenomena as the 12 sense bases – the six internal sense bases [eye, ear, nose, tongue, body, and mind] and the six external sense bases [visible form, sound, odor, taste, tactile object, and mental object] – one can clearly see the impermanence·suffering·non-self. Through this process, one can accomplish the revulsion-dispassion-deliverance-knowledge of liberation and realize the ultimate happiness, Nibbāna. This is the core teaching of the 12 sense bases.

"The Buddha emphasized that the 12 sense bases are 'all conditioned phenomena or the world.' Thus, there are no other phenomena. The world or all conditioned phenomena do not exist without the contact of the six internal and six external sense bases."

The 12 Sense Bases are 'All Conditioned Phenomena'

Let's take a look at the importance of the teaching of the 12 sense bases or the six sense bases. Primarily, the Buddha's clear explanation that the 12 sense bases are all that exist or all conditioned phenomena must be noted. The Buddha taught the 12 sense bases by deconstructing the world into the six internal sense bases [eye, ear, nose, tongue, body, and mind] and the six external sense bases [visible form, sound, odor, taste, tactile object, and mental object]. The Buddha firmly asserted that these are all that exist and there are no other phenomena.

This is what the Buddha said in the Saṁyutta Nikāya:

"And what, bhikkhus, are all conditioned phenomena? The eye and visible forms, the ear and sounds, the nose and odors, the tongue and tastes, the body and tactile objects, the mind and mental objects. This is called the all. If anyone, bhikkhus, should speak thus: 'Having rejected this all, I shall make known another all' – that would be a mere empty boast on his part. If he were questioned he would not be able to reply and, further, he would meet with vexation. For what reason? Because, bhikkhus, that would not be within his domain." (S35:23, the All Discourse)

In this, the Buddha has shown simply and clearly, through the teaching of the 12 sense bases using deconstruction that all conditioned phenomena and the world are the internal and external sense bases.

Why did the Buddha teach by deconstructing the world using the 12 sense bases? To clearly show the impermanence·suffering·non-self, just as he did with the five aggregates. The world or all conditioned phenomena can be confusing since they appear to be permanent, unchanging, everlasting, and absolute. Attachment can arise when all conditioned phenomena are viewed in this way.

But if one deconstructs and sees the world as the 12 sense bases [eye, ear, nose, tongue, body, mind, visible form, sound, odor, taste, tactile object, and mental object], the impermanence·suffering·non-self of the world will be clearly revealed. One will surely know then that eye is impermanent and the eye's object or visible form is also impermanent.

If one sees the impermanence·suffering·non-self, ultimately one will accomplish revulsion-dispassion-deliverance-knowledge of liberation and realize deliverance·Nibbāna. This is the same method used when one deconstructs and sees 'I' as the five aggregates. The path to revulsion-dispassion-deliverance-knowledge of liberation will be clearly revealed through the five aggregates' impermanence·suffering·non-self. In many places within the Early Buddhist discourses, the following is stressed:

> "Bhikkhus, the eye is impermanent ... the mind is impermanent. Seeing thus ... He understands: '... there is no more for this state of being.' Bhikkhus, the eye is suffering ... the mind is suffering. Seeing thus ... He understands: '... there is no more for this state of being.' Bhikkhus, the eye is non-self ... the mind is non-self. Seeing thus ... He understands: '... there is no more for this state of being.'" (S35:222–224, the Bases as Impermanent [internal] Discourse)

One is fooled by the concept of the world and all conditioned phenomena when they are bundled up; one is liberated when the the world and all conditioned phenomena are further deconstructed into the 12 sense bases or the dhammas. One is a true disciple of the Buddha when one can deconstruct and see the world and the all conditioned phenomena as the 12 sense bases.

"If one deconstructs and sees the world as the 12 sense bases [eye, ear, nose, tongue, body, mind, visible form, sound, odor, taste, tactile object, and mental object] the impermanence·suffering·non-self of the world will be clearly revealed."

The 18 Elements

Classifying all conditioned phenomena as the six sensory faculties, the six sense objects, and the six sense consciousnesses constitutes the teaching of the 18 elements [dhatu]. When the six sensory faculties [eye, ear, nose, tongue, body, and mind] or the internal sense bases come in contact with the six sense objects [visible form, sound, odor, taste, tactile object, and mental object] or the external sense bases, connected consciousnesses inevitably arise.

In other words, sense consciousness arises once contact is made between the sensory faculty and the sense object:

Eye consciousness arises from contact between the eye and the visible form, ear consciousness arises from contact between the ear and sound, nose consciousness arises from contact between the nose and odor, tongue consciousness arises from contact between the tongue and taste, body consciousness arises from contact between the body and the tactile object, mind consciousness arises from contact between the mind and the mental object.

Adding these six dependently arisen consciousnesses to the 12 sense bases and classifying them as the 18 elements is called the teaching of the 18 elements.

In discourses, the 18 elements are defined as follows:

"The eye element, visible form element, eye-consciousness element; the ear element, sound element, ear-consciousness element; the nose element, odor element, nose-consciousness element; the tongue element, taste element, tongue-consciousness element; the body element, tactile-object element, body-consciousness element; the mind element, mental-object element, mind-consciousness element." (S14:1, the Diversity of Elements Discourse)

Why did the Buddha explain the 18 elements again in addition to the teaching of the 12 sense bases? Although several reasons can be listed, the most important one pertains to preventing the absolutization of the mind. The teaching of the 18 elements clearly show that mind or consciousness is not an absolute thing but arises in dependence on contact of the internal and external sense bases; the mind or consciousness is nothing but a momentary flow. Dependent origination, Buddhism's basic teaching, has been expanded and transposed here.

About the arising and the passing away of the world, The Buddha said the following:

> "And what, bhikkhus, is the origin of the world? In dependence on the eye and visible forms, eye-consciousness arises. The meeting of the three is contact. With contact as condition, feeling [comes to be]; with feeling as condition, craving; with craving as condition, clinging; with clinging as condition, becoming; with becoming as condition, birth; with birth as condition, aging-and-death, sorrow, lamentation, pain, displeasure, and despair come to be. This, bhikkhus, is the origin of the world." (S35:107, the Origin of the World Discourse)

The Buddha explained the passing away of the world using the same method. In many places within the Early Buddhist discourses, it is emphasized that the world is only a dependently-originated state based on the consciousness arisen from contact of the internal and external sense bases. The teaching of the 18 elements shows clearly that, without the internal and external sense bases, there is no such thing as an independent mind or consciousness. Therefore, in the commentaries, it is explained that the 18 elements are merely a name to show that "all conditioned phenomena such as sentient beings, soul, and so forth are empty and have no-self." (SA.ii.131)

"The teaching of the 18 elements shows that mind or consciousness is not an absolute thing but instead is dependently originated from contact of the internal and external sense bases and is only a momentary flow."

The 22 Faculties of Human Beings

The 22 faculties refer to the 22 powers of human beings. Human beings have unique powers. For example, seeing, feeling, thinking, and the realization of Nibbāna are some of those tremendous powers. In the Early Buddhist discourses, the Buddha established that there are 22 human faculties [indriya]. These faculties appear in 178 discourses within the Indriyasaṁyutta of Saṁyutta Nikāya.

The 22 faculties are: 1) eye, 2) ear, 3) nose, 4) tongue, 5) body, 6) mind, 7) femininity, 8) masculinity 9) life, 10) bodily pleasure, 11) bodily pain, 12) mental joy, 13) mental grief, 14) equanimity, 15) faith, 16) energy, 17) mindfulness, 18) concentration, 19) understanding [wisdom], 20) 'I shall-come-to-know-the-unknown,' 21) final-knowledge, and 22) final-knower. (Vis. XVI.A.1)

Indriya is translated as 'faculty' and Indra, herein, is the king of gods who appears many times in India's Veda and Buddhist literature. In Chinese this is written as 帝釋 [Indra] and is well known to Koreans. Like Indra, the mark of a ruler [inda], Indriya's meaning is 'rulership' or faculty. Therefore, these 22 faculties are the mental phenomena that dominate the dhammas related to each respective area of the 22 faculties.

The 22 faculties listed above are made up of five parts: 1) six sensory faculties, 2) three special faculties, 3) five feeling faculties, 4) five faculties to achieve deliverance·Nibbāna, and 5) three faculties possessed by the noble ones who achieved the eight stages of attainment.

Let's briefly examine the above-listed faculties.

1. The six sensory faculties: As only the eye can see and only the ear can hear, each of the six sensory faculties [eye, ear, nose, tongue, body, and mind] has its own unique capability, faculty, and skill. Therefore, eye, ear, etc. are called eye-vision and ear-hearing faculties, and so forth.

2. The three special faculties: "The femininity faculty exercises

control over femininity [i.e., determines the distinctive feminine features of a female]; the masculinity faculty exercises control over masculinity. The life faculty [jīvitindriya] is another type of derivative form, responsible for maintaining conascent mental and physical phenomena." (S48:22:205, the Indriyasaṃyutta Discourse)

3. The five feeling faculties: The feeling faculty also possesses unique characteristics. In the discourses feeling is classified into three categories – pleasant, painful, and neutral. These are further categorized into five types – physical pleasure, physical pain, mental joy, mental grief, and equanimity.

4. The five faculties to achieve deliverance·Nibbāna are faith, energy, mindfulness, concentration, and wisdom.

5. The three faculties possessed by the noble ones [those who have realized the eight stages of attainment from the path of stream-entry to the fruition of Arahantship] are the faculty 'I shall-come-to-know-the-unknown,' the faculty of final knowledge, and the faculty of final-knower. The faculty 'I shall-come-to-know-the-unknown' arises at the moment one experiences the path of stream-entry. The faculty of final knowledge arises to the noble ones who have realized six stages of attainment from the fruition of stream-entry to the path of Arahantship. The faculty of final knower arises to noble ones who have realized the fruition of Arahantship.

These 22 faculties are all important, but only the five faculties [faith, energy, mindfulness, concentration, and wisdom] and the identical five powers are mentioned in the 37 requisites of enlightenment. The five faculties will be examined in detail later.

"The Buddha said the 22 faculties are the power and faculties of human beings. These 22 faculties are the mental phenomena that dominate the dhammas related to each of the 22 faculties' respective areas."

The Six Stages of Teaching to Attain Deliverance·Nibbāna

Previously, the five aggregates, the 12 sense bases, and the 18 elements have been reviewed. The five aggregates are about deconstructing and explaining 'I' as material form, feeling, perception, mental formations, and consciousness. The 12 sense bases are about deconstructing and explaining 'the world' as eye, ear, nose, tongue, body, mind, visible form, sound, odor, taste, tactile object, and mental object. The mind among the 12 sense bases is further deconstructed as eye, ear, nose, tongue, body, and mind consciousness and explained as the 18 elements. These are Buddhism's fundamental teachings.

Why is deconstruction emphasized? Because only by deconstructing and seeing, can one realize deliverance·Nibbāna. The method of deconstructing and seeing to realize deliverance·Nibbāna is explained in various places in the Early Buddhist discourses. There are six stages:

1. deconstructing and seeing the conditioned phenomena as the five aggregates, the 12 sense bases, and the 18 elements
2. having a firm view of the impermanence·suffering·non-self of the conditioned phenomena
3. experiencing revulsion [nibbidā]
4. experiencing dispassion [virāga]
5. attaining deliverance [vimutti]
6. attaining knowledge of liberation [vimuttamiti ñāṇa]

Let's take a closer look at these six stages.

First, the Buddha explained all conditioned phenomena such as 'I' and 'the world,' by deconstructing them into the five aggregates, the 12 sense bases, and the 18 elements. Why did he explain by deconstructing all conditioned phenomena into dhammas? Because when one deconstructs and sees the dhamma, the impermanence·suffering·non-self becomes visible.

Second, to realize deliverance·Nibbāna one must deconstruct and see the impermanence·suffering·non-self of all conditioned phenomena. When conceptual beings are left bundled up, the impermanence·suffering·non-self cannot be seen.

For example, when 'I' is left as a conceptual being like the self, the true self, or a sentient being, it seems that an eternal non-changing self exists. But when these are deconstructed as material form, feeling, perception, mental formations, and consciousness [the five aggregates], the impermanence·suffering·non-self becomes readily visible.

All conditioned phenomena have these three characteristics [tilakkhana] – the impermanence·suffering·non-self. It is emphasized in the *Dhammapada* that, "all created things perish, all created things are grief and pain, and all forms are unreal." (Dhp. 277–279)

The nature of these dhammas – impermanence·suffering·non-self – is called the general characteristic [sāmañña-lakkhaṇa] in the Abhidhamma and the Northern Abhidharma. It is translated as the shared characteristic 共相 in Chinese. It is the common view of all Buddhism throughout history that one realizes deliverance·Nibbāna by seeing all conditioned phenomena's general or shared characteristics, impermanence·suffering·non-self.

Third, by seeing the impermanence·suffering·non-self, one experiences revulsion towards all conditioned phenomena. In many places in the Early Buddhist discourses, it is said, "Seeing thus, bhikkhus, the instructed noble disciple experiences revulsion towards material form, revulsion towards feeling, revulsion towards perception, revulsion towards mental formations, revulsion towards consciousness." (S22:59) It is explained this revulsion is synonymous with the intense vipassanā in commentaries. (MA. ii.115)

Fourth, when revulsion arises, dispassion follows. The commentaries explain, "Dispassion is the path [magga] of stream-entry, once-returning, non-returning, and Arahantship." (MA. ii.115)

Fifth, dispassion leads to deliverance. The commentaries explain that this is the fruition [phala] of stream-entry, once-returning, non-returning, and Arahantship. (MA.ii.115)

Sixth, when one is liberated, the knowledge that one is liberated arises. The Early Buddhist discourses standardized the steps from revulsion to knowledge of liberation as follows:

> "Seeing thus, bhikkhus, the instructed noble disciple experiences revulsion towards [material] form, revulsion towards feeling, revulsion towards perception, revulsion towards mental formations, revulsion towards consciousness. Experiencing revulsion, he becomes dispassionate. Through dispassion [his mind] is liberated. When it is liberated there comes the knowledge: 'It's liberated.' He understands: 'Destroyed is birth, the holy life has been lived, what had to be done has been done, there is no more for this state of being.'" (S22:59, The Characteristic of Non-Self Discourse)

These six stages to realize deliverance·Nibbāna are the central teachings of the Early Buddhist discourses. All Buddhism of later generations, albeit in differing degrees of emphases, have accepted this standardization.

"The teaching of the six stages that leads to the realization of deliverance·Nibbāna is to deconstruct and see all conditioned phenomena as the five aggregates, the 12 sense bases, the 18 elements and to have a firm view of the impermanence·suffering·non-self which leads to revulsion-dispassion-deliverance-knowledge of liberation."

❧ CHAPTER 4
What is the Truth?

The Four Noble Truths:
Four Kinds of Noble Truths

All philosophies, ideologies, and religions of the world stand for the truth. Of course, Buddhism also stands for the truth. In Buddhism, there are four truths which are emphasized, and these are called 'the Four Noble Truths.' The Pāli words for the Four Noble Truths are cattari ariya-saccāni.

Here, the word 'ariya' is translated as 'noble.' Ariya is attached only to the Four Noble Truths which is one of the six subjects of the Buddhist theory [the five aggregates, the 12 sense bases, the 18 elements, the 22 faculties, the Four Noble Truths, and the 12 links of dependent origination].

Also, ariya is attached only to the noble eightfold path which is one of the seven subjects of the 37 requisites of enlightenment [the four foundations of mindfulness, the four right efforts, the four bases for spiritual power, the five faculties, the five powers, the seven factors of enlightenment, and the noble eightfold path].

The content of 'the way leading to the cessation of suffering' among the Four Noble Truths is the noble eightfold path. Therefore, the noble eightfold path is included in the Four Noble Truths. Because the four kinds of truth are the noblest and most sacred teaching, the descriptive word 'ariya' is used and they are thus called the Four Noble Truths.

Venerable Sāriputta asserted all teachings of the Buddha can be included in the Four Noble Truths as follows:

> "Friends, just as the footprint of any living being that walks can be placed within an elephant's footprint, and so the elephant's footprint is declared the chief of them because of its great size; so too, all wholesome states can be included in the Four Noble Truths." (M28, The Greater Discourse on the Simile of the Elephant's Footprint)

The direct translation of the Four Noble Truths, as appeared in the Early Buddhist discourses, are as follows:

1. The noble truth of suffering: dukkha ariya-sacca
2. The noble truth of the origin of suffering: dukkha-samudaya ariya-sacca
3. The noble truth of the cessation of suffering: dukkha-nirodha ariya-sacca
4. The noble truth of the way leading to the cessation of suffering: dukkha-nirodha-gāmini-paṭipadā ariya-sacca

As seen here, the four kinds of truth of the Nikāyas are all based on the reality of suffering. Therefore, the word, 'suffering' is included in all four kinds of truth and standardized as the noble truth of suffering, the noble truth of the origin of suffering, the noble truth of the cessation of suffering, and the noble truth of the way leading to the cessation of suffering. The *Āgama Discourse* translation also includes the word, 'suffering' [the noble truth of the origin of suffering, the noble truth of the cessation of suffering, and the noble truth of the way leading to the cessation of suffering]. However, in the Mahāyāna discourses, such as in the Paññā section, there are far more expressions without the word, 'suffering' [the noble truth of the origin, the noble truth of the cessation, and the noble truth of the way leading to the cessation]. In the later generations, 'noble' has been removed and expressed in an abridged fashion [the truth of suffering, the truth of the origin, the truth of the cessation, and the truth of the way leading to the cessation].

The Four Noble Truths are the basic subject of the *Saccasaṁyutta Discourse* [the Connected Discourses on the Truths], the great finale of the Saṁyutta Nikāya, which is a collection of the Buddha's teachings by subject matter. The *Saccasaṁyutta Discourse*, which includes 131 discourses, emphasizes that the reason for developing concentration (S56:1) and becoming a monastic (S56:3–4) is to penetrate the Four Noble Truths. Furthermore, when one reflects and speaks, one should always reflect and speak about the Four Noble Truths. (S56:8) "It is because he has fully awakened to these Four Noble Truths as they really are that the Tathāgata is called the Arahant, the Perfectly Enlightened One." (S56:23) It is also emphasized, "The destruction of the taints comes about for one who knows and sees." (S56:25) In the various discourses of the *Saccasaṁyutta Discourse*, the importance of the Four Noble Truths has been asserted.

The Buddha explains why he is the enlightened one:

> "What is to be comprehended [the noble truth of suffering] is comprehended by me; what is to be developed [the noble truth of the way leading to the cessation of suffering] is developed by me; what is to be abandoned [the noble truth of the origin of suffering] has been abandoned by me. Therefore, O Brahmin, I am Buddha." (Sn.558, the Nipāta Discourse)

"All the teachings of the Buddha can be included in the Four Noble Truths. Because he has fully awakened to the Four Noble Truths, he is called the Tathāgata, the Arahant, and the Perfectly Enlightened One. The destruction of the taints comes about for one who knows and sees."

The Four Noble Truths:
The Noble Truth of Suffering

Among the Four Noble Truths, the first truth is 'the noble truth of suffering [dukkha ariya-sacca].' In Buddhism, except for Nibbāna – the unconditioned, it is understood that all conditioned phenomena are suffering. This is what the Buddha proclaimed. The Early Buddhist discourses describe the suffering of all conditioned phenomena for two reasons.

First, there are the four and eight kinds of suffering in the world. The various discourses of Nikāyas standardized the four and eight kinds of suffering as follows:

> "Now this, bhikkhus, is the noble truth of suffering: birth is suffering, aging is suffering, illness is suffering, death is suffering; union with what is displeasing is suffering; separation from what is pleasing is suffering; not to get what one wants is suffering; in brief, the five aggregates subject to clinging are suffering." (S56:11, the Setting in Motion the Wheel of the Dhamma Discourse)

As seen in the above discourse, the four kinds of suffering are birth, aging, illness, and death. The eight kinds of suffering are the previous four kinds of suffering plus the following four kinds of suffering: union with what is displeasing, separation from what is pleasing, not to get what one wants, and the five aggregates subject to clinging. In summation, 'the five aggregates subject to clinging are suffering' includes the four and eight kinds of suffering. Remember, the being 'I' is composed of the five aggregates. Sentient beings cling to these five aggregates as 'I' and 'mine.' Therefore, our lives, composed of the five aggregates have to be suffering. The four and eight kinds of suffering are, in short, a matter of life and death. It is suffering because birth and death occur.

Second, in several places within the Early Buddhist discourses, it is explained that all conditioned phenomena are suffering and have three characteristics:

> "Friend Sāriputta, it is said, 'suffering, suffering.' What now is suffering?"

> "There are, friend, these three kinds of suffering: suffering due to pain, suffering due to change, suffering due to formations. These are the three kinds of suffering." (S38:14, the Suffering Discourse)

The suffering due to pain means that sentient beings' lives are painful. Therefore, there is suffering. The suffering due to change means that no matter how great happiness may be, it will inevitably change. Therefore, there is suffering. The suffering due to formations means one clings to 'I' and 'mine' that are simply composed of the five aggregates. Therefore, there is suffering. These three points are explained in the Path of Purification:

> "Herein, bodily and mental painful feeling are called *intrinsic suffering* because of their individual essence, their name, and their painfulness. [Bodily and mental] pleasant feeling are called *suffering in change* because they are a cause for the arising of pain when they change. (M.i,303) Equanimous feeling and the remaining formations of the three spheres are called *suffering due to formations* because they are oppressed by arising and passing away." (Vis.XVI.35)

Suffering due to formations means 'the five aggregates subject to clinging are suffering' among the eight kinds of suffering. So, except for Nibbāna – the unconditioned, all conditioned phenomena are suffering due to these three characteristics. Because suffering is emphasized in Buddhism, some may criticize Buddhism as being pessimistic. If Buddhism only talks about suffering, such criticism would have been well deserved. But the reason for emphasizing suffering in Buddhism is that suffering can be resolved. Greater consideration is given to the realization of the ultimate happiness, Nibbāna.

One cannot realize the happiness of deliverance Nibbāna when one is not deeply concerned about the fact that existence is suffering.

"The first truth of the Four Noble Truths, the noble truth of suffering means the five aggregates subject to clinging are suffering. There are the four and eight kinds of suffering in the world. All conditioned phenomena have three characteristics of suffering."

The Four Noble Truths: The Noble Truth of the Origin of Suffering

Does suffering arise spontaneously? If it does not arise spontaneously, does that mean an almighty god is torturing beings? If suffering is emphasized and no explanation for the cause of suffering is given, it cannot be called the truth. Hence, the second truth of the Four Noble Truths explains why suffering arises and what the cause of suffering is. This is called 'the noble truth of the origin of suffering [dukkha-samudaya ariya-sacca].' The Pāli word samudaya means arising, origin, or cause. In Chinese, samudaya is translated as 集.

The Buddha expounded about the cause for the origin of suffering in many places in the Early Buddhist discourses. The cause of suffering is craving [taṇhā]. Taṇhā's literal meaning is 'thirst.' In Chinese it is translated as 渴愛 [thirst]. The discourses define craving as follows:

> "Now this, bhikkhus, is the noble truth of the origin of suffering:
> it is this craving which leads to renewed existence, accompanied by delight and lust, seeking delight here and there; that
> is, craving for sensual pleasures, craving for existence, craving
> for extermination." (S56:11, the Setting in Motion the Wheel
> of the Dhamma Discourse)

The Buddha expounded that craving is the fundamental cause leading to rebirth or renewed existence. This deserves special attention. Because of craving, sentient beings repeat the cycle of birth and death. Of course, craving is not the sole cause of suffering. The unwholesome dhammas such as ignorance, anger, envy, stinginess, etc. are also causes for suffering and the endless cycle of birth and death; nevertheless, the Buddha said craving is the most important cause. Here the phrase 'accompanied by delight and lust' shows that craving and 'delight and lust' have the same meaning. (DA.iii.799)

The Buddha talked about the three kinds of craving: kāma-taṇhā, bhava-taṇhā, and vibhava-taṇhā. Kāma-taṇhā is craving for sensual pleasures. The commentaries explain that kāma-taṇhā is 'a synonym for the lust of the five cords of sensual pleasure.' (DA.iii.800) The lust for the objects perceived through the five sense organs [eye, ear, nose, tongue, and body] is called kāma-taṇhā. This craving occurs each and every moment to us, because we live in the sensual-desire sphere[1].

Bhava-taṇhā is craving for the form and formless spheres. Bhava-taṇhā – together with the eternalism caused by the desire for existence – is a synonym for lust for existence in the form and formless spheres and craving for jhāna.' (DA.iii.800)

The form and formless spheres are the spheres one is born into through the practice of jhāna. Therefore, arousing an intense craving for jhāna practice and absorption concentration, so that one can be born into the form and formless spheres, is called bhava-taṇhā.

Vibhava-taṇhā is craving for non-existence and a synonym of craving for annihilationism. (DA.iii.800) Vibhava-taṇhā means feeling disgusted with existence, possibly causing the impulse to commit suicide, for instance. I think perhaps greater vibhava-taṇhā exists among contemporary human beings because of their intense feelings of disgust and despair about their complicated lives and relationships. However, vibhava-taṇhā, craving for extermination, is a definite kind of craving.

As long as a craving exists, regardless of the type, sentient beings will be reborn. If one definitely does not want to be reborn, one must realize Nibbāna, a state of complete extinguishment of cravings [kāma-taṇhā, bhava-taṇhā, and vibhava-taṇhā].

---

1 The sensual-desire sphere is one of the three spheres in Buddhist cosmology.

"The noble truth of the origin of suffering, the second truth of the Four Noble Truths means 'craving.' The Buddha said craving is the foremost cause of the cycle of rebirth."

The Four Noble Truth: The Noble Truth of the Cessation of Suffering

The third of the Four Noble Truths is 'the noble truth of the cessation of suffering [dukkha-nirodha ariya-sacca].' The second truth, the noble truth of the origin of suffering, is craving. If craving is the cause of suffering, one arrives at a conclusion that suffering will cease by the removal of craving. Thus, the cessation of suffering is the third truth, which means Nibbāna.

The Early Buddhist discourses and the commentaries explain the third truth as follows:

> "Now this, bhikkhus, is the noble truth of the cessation of suffering: it is the remainderless fading away and cessation of that same craving, the giving up and relinquishing of it, free from it, nonreliance on it." (S56:11, the Setting in Motion the Wheel of the Dhamma Discourse)

Here, 'the remainderless fading away and cessation' is synonymous with Nibbāna. When Nibbāna is realized, craving becomes remainderless through fading away and cessation. (DA.iii.801)

In the Early Buddhist discourses, the third truth, cessation [nirodha] is synonymous with Nibbāna and means suppression, destruction, etc.

Nibbāna means 'a state of extinguished fire.' In Chinese it is transliterated as 涅槃 [Nie-pan] and translated as 寂靜 [Nibbāna].

What is extinguished? And by what? Venerable Sāriputta clearly explained as follows:

> "Friend Sāriputta, it is said, 'Nibbāna, Nibbāna.' What now is Nibbāna?"

> "The destruction of lust, the destruction of hatred, the destruction of delusion: this friend, is called Nibbāna." (S38:1, A Question on Nibbāna Discourse)

As explained here, Nibbāna is a state of complete extinguishment of the three poisons: lust, hatred, and delusion. To summarize the discussions of the commentaries, Nibbāna is explained as 'a state of the unconditioned' that is comprehended at the moment one experiences the supramundane path[2] [lokuttara-magga].

Nibbāna is not a weak and lethargic state due to simple cessation of lust, hatred, and delusion. Nibbāna is called 'the destruction of lust, the destruction of hatred, and the destruction of delusion' since the cessation of taints occurs at the moment of comprehension of the state of the unconditioned. (SA.ii.88)

Early Buddhism's ultimate message is Nibbāna. In short, Nibbāna is realized by abandoning. Nibbāna appears when all that we belive life to mean [represented with lust, hatred, and delusion] is destroyed.

If the Buddha who was sick of the world overflowing with lust, hatred, and delusion said to realize Nibbāna, shouldn't a rightful disciple strive to do so?

"The third truth, the noble truth of the cessation of suffering is 'Nibbāna.' By eliminating craving, the cause of suffering, one can arrive at the state of Nibbāna, where all suffering is extinguished."

---

2 The supramundane path [lokuttara-magga] – The term 'supramundane' applies exclusively to that which transcends the world. There are nine supramundane states: Nibbāna, the four noble paths [magga] leading to Nibbāna, and their corresponding fruits [phala] which experience the bliss of Nibbāna.

The Four Noble Truths: The Noble Truth of the Way Leading to the Cessation of Suffering

The last of the Four Noble Truths is 'the noble truth of the way leading to the cessation of suffering [dukkha-nirodha-gāmini-paṭipadā ariya-sacca].' This is well known as the noble truth of the path. As previously stated, the third truth, the noble truth of the cessation of suffering, is Nibbāna. The Buddha emphasized that Nibbāna is the ultimate happiness. So, how is Nibbāna realized?

Nibbāna is realized by practicing the noble eightfold path. The following is stated in the discourses:

> "And what, friend, is that path, what is that way for the realization of this Nibbāna?"

> "It is, friend, this noble eightfold path; that is, right view, right intention, right speech, right action, right livelihood, right effort, right mindfulness, and right concentration." (S38:1, A Question on Nibbāna Discourse)

Let's examine several aspects of the noble eightfold path. First, the Buddha talks about the noble eightfold path in the *Setting in Motion the Wheel of the Dhamma Discourse*, his first discourse after his enlightenment. He states the following:

> "And what bhikkhus, is that middle path awakened to by the Tathāgata, which gives rise to vision, which gives rise to knowledge, which leads to peace, to direct knowledge, to enlightenment, to Nibbāna? It is this noble eightfold path; that is, right view, right intention, right speech, right action, right livelihood, right effort, right mindfulness, and right concentration." (S56:11, the Setting in Motion the Wheel of the Dhamma Discourse)

Second, the Buddha discusses the noble eightfold path in his last discourse. Stated in the *Great Passing Discourse* [the Mahāparinibbāna Discourse] is the following:

76

"In whatever Dhamma and discipline the noble eightfold path is not found, no samaṇa[3] is found of the first, the second, the third, or the fourth grade. But such samaṇas can be found of the first, second, third, and fourth grade in Dhamma and discipline where the noble eightfold path is found. Now Subbadha, in this Dhamma and discipline the noble eightfold path is found, and in it are to be found samaṇas of the first, second, third, and fourth grade. Those other schools are devoid of [true] samaṇas" (D16, the Mahāparinibbāna Discourse)

Third, the noble eightfold path represents the practice. The word 'path' or 'way' appears with two meanings: path [magga] and walking the path or practicing [paṭipadā]. Specifically the path contained in 'the noble eightfold path' is a translation of magga. The way in 'the noble truth of the way leading to the cessation of suffering' and the path in 'the middle path [majjhimā paṭipadā]' are a translation of the practice [paṭipadā]. Here paṭipadā is a very important technical term with a strong inference to the 'practice' and literally means stepping and walking [padā] on the path [paṭi].

The important fact is that, as explained in the *Setting in Motion the Wheel of the Dhamma Discourse*, the noble eightfold path is the middle path [majjhimā paṭipadā]. When we think of the middle path, we first think of the *Eight Negations of the Middle Way* taught by the Venerable Nāgârjuna [a.k.a. Bhikkhu Yongsu in Korea]. However, in the Early Buddhist discourses, the middle path always appears as the noble eightfold path. Therefore, the middle path should not be viewed only as the interpretation and philosophy of such things as the *Eight Negations of the Middle Way*. Since the middle path means the noble eightfold path in the Early Buddhist discourses – the root of Buddhism, the middle

---

3 Samaṇa refers to recluse, monk, or ascetic.

path is the 'practice.' One must first accept the Buddha's sincere explanation of the noble eightfold path as the practice system.

Each category of the noble eightfold path will be explained in detail later in this book while covering the noble eightfold path among the 37 requisites of enlightenment.

"The fourth truth of the Four Noble Truths, the noble truth of the way leading to the cessation of suffering, is the noble eightfold path. Nibbāna can be realized through practicing the noble eightfold path."

The Four Noble Truths: Taking the Four Noble Truths to Heart

All teachings of Buddhism ultimately are contained in the Four Noble Truths. The understanding about 'I' and 'the world' is the content of the first of the Four Noble Truths – the noble truth of suffering. Therefore, the teachings of the five aggregates, the 12 sense bases, and the 18 elements are included in the Four Noble Truths.

The forward order [anuloma] of the 12 links of dependent origination is both the noble truth of suffering and the noble truth of the origin of suffering. The reverse order [paṭiloma] of the 12 links of dependent origination is both the noble truth of the cessation of suffering and the noble truth of the way leading to the cessation of suffering. Therefore, the forward order and reverse order of the 12 links of dependent origination are contained in the Four Noble Truths.

The right view, the first of the noble eightfold path, is knowing the Four Noble Truths. The noble eightfold path is also the fourth of the Four Noble Truths – the noble truth of the way leading to the cessation of suffering. The noble eightfold path is contained in the Four Noble Truths. The Four Noble Truths and the noble eightfold path contain each other. Thus, the practice is contained in the theory and the theory is contained in the practice or the theory and the practice are intertwined and coexist.

The Buddha's first discourse, the *Setting in Motion the Wheel of the Dhamma Discourse,* is the proclamation of the Four Noble Truths and the noble eightfold path.

The Four Noble Truths also contain the content of realization. The last of the six supernormal powers,[4] the knowledge of the destruction of the taints, is included in the Four Noble Truths.

---

4 The six supernormal powers are developed based on the fourth jhāna.

"And he with mind concentrated, purified and cleansed, unblemished, free from impurities, malleable, workable, established and having gained imperturbability, applies and directs his mind to the knowledge of the destruction of the taints. He knows as it really is: 'This is suffering,' he knows as it really is: 'This is the origin of suffering,' he knows as it really is; 'This is the cessation of suffering,' he knows as it really is: 'This is the path leading to the cessation of suffering.' And he knows as it really is: 'These are the taints,' 'This is the origin of the taints,' 'This is the cessation of the taints,' 'This is the path leading to the cessation of the taints.'

"And through his knowing and seeing, his mind is delivered from the corruption of sense-desire, from the corruption of becoming, from the corruption of ignorance, and the knowledge arises in him: 'This is deliverance!' and he knows: 'Birth is finished, the holy life has been led, done is what had to be done, there is nothing further here.'" (D2, the Fruits of the Homeless Life Discourse)

All teachings of Buddhism are contained in the Four Noble Truths. Therefore, all schools of Buddhism claim these four as the noble truths. Buddhists must take these four truths to heart.

The Buddha said, "And what, bhikkhus, is the noble truth that is to be fully understood? The noble truth of suffering is to be fully understood; the noble truth of the origin of suffering is to be abandoned; the noble truth of the cessation of suffering is to be realized; the noble truth of the way leading to the cessation of suffering is to be developed." (S56:29, the To Be Fully Understood Discourse)

One must know clearly and thoroughly the suffering of the five aggregates. The Abhidhamma throughly analizes all conditioned phenomena's suffering as if hollowing out a groove in a strand of hair. Likewise, one must know clearly by deconstructing all conditioned phenomena into dhammas. Craving, the foremost reason for suffering, must be discarded, thrown away, and completely extinguished. We must, here and now realize Nibbāna, a state of complete freedom from suffering. Nibbāna can be realized here and now by practicing the noble eightfold path.

In short, one must take each truth of the Four Noble Truths to heart. When one takes suffering to heart, one becomes desperate to be free of suffering. Only when one takes suffering to heart, does one become disgusted with sticky craving, the cause of the suffering. Then one would want to be free from suffering. One takes the nobleness of Nibbāna to heart by knowing the bottomless pit of craving with extreme sadness. When one treats Nibbāna as one's reason for living, one takes Nibbāna to heart. Then one will take the practice of the noble eightfold path to heart for the realization of Nibbāna.

The Buddha sincerely expounded as follows:

"These are the feet of trees, bhikkhus, these are empty huts. Meditate, bhikkhus, do not be negligent, lest you regret it later. This is our instruction to you." (S43:1, the Mindfulness Directed to the Body Discourse)

Following the Buddha's sincere plea, all Buddhists must practice the noble eightfold path to realize deliverance·Nibbāna through 'the knowledge of the destruction of the taints' – the insight of the Four Noble Truths.

"The noble truth of suffering is to be fully understood; the noble truth of the origin of suffering is to be abandoned; the noble truth of the cessation of suffering is to be realized; the noble truth of the way leading to the cessation of suffering is to be developed." (S56:29, the To Be Fully Understood Discourse)

🦎 CHAPTER 5

What is Dependent Origination?

Dependent Origination:
The 12 Links of Dependent Origination

The origin of the technical term 'dependent origination,' is paṭicca-samuppāda. Here, paṭicca means 'depend on something.' Samuppāda's literal meaning is 'go up together,' and could mean arising, occurring, or originating. It has been translated as 緣起 [origin] in Chinese. It is translated as 조건발생 [conditional occurence] in Korean.

When circumstances arise because of certain conditions, are they then dependently originated? For example, a mother and father have a son. Are these familial relationships dependently originated? According to the Early Buddhist discourses, they are not.

In the Early Buddhist discourses, various dependent originations, from two to 12 links appear. These all show the origin [anuloma] and cessation [paṭiloma] of suffering and are called dependent origination. Otherwise, phenomena's interrelations or interdependence are not called dependent origination but are called paccaya, or more specifically, paṭṭhāna in the Abhidhamma.

The teaching of dependent origination mostly appears as the standardized 12 links of dependent origination. In the Early Buddhist discourses, the 12 links of dependent origination appear without exception in the following standardized format:

"With ignorance as condition, volitional formations [come to be]; with volitional formations as condition, consciousness; with consciousness as condition, name-and-form[1]; with name-and-form as condition, the six sense bases; with the six sense bases as condition, contact; with contact as condition, feeling; with feeling as condition, craving; with craving as condition, clinging; with clinging as condition, becoming; with becoming as condition, birth; with birth as condition, aging-and-death, sorrow, lamentation, pain, displeasure, and despair come to be. Such is the origin of this whole mass of suffering.

"But with the remainderless fading away and cessation of ignorance comes cessation of volitional formations; with the cessation of volitional formations, cessation of consciousness; with the cessation of consciousness, cessation of name-and-form; with the cessation of name-and-form, cessation of the six sense bases; with the cessation of the six sense bases, cessation of contact; with the cessation of contact, cessation of feeling; with the cessation of feeling, cessation of craving; with the cessation of craving, cessation of clinging; with the cessation of clinging, cessation of becoming; with the cessation of becoming, cessation of birth; with the cessation of birth, aging-and-death, sorrow, lamentation, pain, displeasure, and despair cease. Such is the cessation of this whole mass of suffering." (S12:1, the Dependent Origination Discourse)

---

1 Name and form [nāma-rūpa] refers to mind and body.

In other words, only the 12 links from ignorance, volitional formations to birth, and aging-and-death, or the condensed versions of the 11, ten, nine ... two links of dependent origination are called dependent origination.

Thus, dependent origination, the 12 links of dependent origination – from ignorance to aging-and-death – is the explanation of the origin and cessation of suffering. This agrees with the truth of Buddhism – the Four Noble Truths [the suffering, the origin of suffering, the cessation of suffering, and the way leading to the cessation of suffering].

"In the Early Buddhist discourses, dependent origination is the teaching of the origin and cessation of suffering, represented as the 12 links of dependent origination from ignorance to aging-and-death."

Dependent Origination: The Origin and Cessation of Suffering

The Buddha said the teaching of dependent origination is "deep and deep in implications." He said, "It is because of not understanding and not penetrating this Dhamma, Ānanda, that this generation has become like a tangled skein, like a knotted ball of thread, like matted reeds and rushes, and does not pass beyond the plane of misery, the bad destinations, the nether world, saṃsāra." (S12:60, the Causation Discourse)

The teaching of dependent origination appears in many places in the Nikāyas and especially in the *Connected Discourses on Causation* of the Saṃyutta Nikāya which contains 72 discourses. These 72 discourses contain 11 kinds of dependent origination arranged in two, three, four, five, six, seven, eight, nine, ten, 11, and 12 links of dependent origination. Here, the two links of dependent origination are the teaching that contains two links, suffering and contact (S12:25); the 12 links of dependent origination are the teaching that contain 12 links, from ignorance, volitional formations, birth to aging-and-death. (S12:1)

In the previous chapter, it was emphasized that dependent origination is basically the teaching of the origin and cessation of suffering. Explaining it in further detail, suffering of the 12 links of dependent origination is suffering resulting from the cycle of rebirth. Therefore, the 12 links of dependent origination can be defined as 'the origin and cessation of suffering caused by the cycle of rebirth.'

The 12 links of the 12 links of dependent origination are: ignorance [avijjā], volitional formations [saṅkhārā], consciousness [viññāṇa], name-and-form [nāma-rūpa], the six sense bases [saḷ-āyatana], contact [phassa], feeling [vedanā], craving [taṇhā], clinging [upādāna], becoming [bhava], birth [jāti], and aging-

and-death [jarā-maraṇa], sorrow, lamentation, pain, displeasure, and despair.

Based on the *Analysis of Dependent Origination Discourse* (S12:2), brief explanations of these 12 links are as follows:

1. Ignorance is defined as not knowing suffering, not knowing the origin of suffering, not knowing the cessation of suffering, and not knowing the way leading to the cessation of suffering. Ignorance, the basic cause of the cycle of rebirth, is being ignorant about the Four Noble Truths. When one becomes an Arahant by penetrating the Four Noble Truths, ignorance will be extinguished.

2. There are three volitional formations [the body, speech, and mind], the chief characteristic of which is the formations of kamma.

3. Consciousness is explained as a pile of six types of consciousness [eye, ear, nose, tongue, body, and mind]. This consciousness is the rebirth-consciousness, the first consciousness of one lifetime.

4. The 'name' in name-and-form [mind and body] refers to feeling, perception, and the three mental formations [volition, contact, and attention]. The reason for mentioning only these three among the mental formations is that they exist even when the mind is very subtle. (SA.ii.16–17) Therefore, in the context of dependent origination, the 'name' in name-and-form, refers to the three aggregates [feeling, perception, and mental formations] but excludes consciousness. Generally, consciousness is included in name but not in dependent origination's name-and-form. The reason for this is that consciousness already appears independently as the third component of the 12 links of dependent origination. (Vbh.147) The word 'form' refers to the four basic elements and the form derived from them.

5. The six sense bases are: eye, ear, nose, tongue, body, and mind.

6. Contact is defined in six classes: eye, ear, nose, tongue, body, and mind.

7. Feeling is defined in six classes: feelings born of eye, ear, nose, tongue, body, and mind.

8. There are six classes of craving: craving for visible forms, sounds, odors, tastes, tactile objects, and mental objects. Craving is the second of the Four Noble Truths, the noble truth of the origin of suffering.

9. There are four kinds of clinging: clinging to sensual pleasures, wrong views, rules and ritual, and to a doctrine of self.

10. There are three kinds of existence: sensual-desire sphere existence, form sphere existence, and formless sphere existence. The commentaries further explain these three kinds of existence as two types of becoming: kamma-process becoming [業有] and rebirth-process becoming [生有]. (SA.ii.14) Greater detail on this topic is available in the Path of Purification. (Vis. XVII.250–251)

11. Birth is defined as "The birth of the various sentient beings into the various orders of sentient beings, their being born, descent [into the womb], production, the manifestation of the aggregates, the obtaining of the sense bases." (S12:2, the Analysis of Dependent Origination Discourse) Birth here means a sentient being born into one lifetime and must not be understood as the arising of 'the arising and passing away.'

12. Aging-and-death is defined as "The aging of the various sentient beings in the various orders of sentient beings, their growing old, brokenness of teeth, grayness of hair, wrinkling of skin, decline of vitality, degeneration of the faculties: this is called aging. The passing away of the various sentient beings from the various orders of sentient beings, their perishing, breakup, disappearance, mortality, death, completion of time, the breakup of the aggregates, the laying down of the carcass:

this is called death." (S12:2, the Analysis of Dependent Origination Discourse)

The commentaries called the first stock phrase of the 12 links of dependent origination [the origin of suffering from birth to aging-and-death] – the forward order [anuloma], and the second stock phrase [the cessation of suffering] – the reverse order [paṭiloma].

Here, the reason suffering has to be seen as 'suffering from the cycle of rebirth' is that in the Early Buddhist discourses, without exception, birth [the 11th of the 12 links of dependent origination] means the birth of a sentient being into one lifetime. Birth here does not refer to the arising of the arising and passing away [udaya-vaya]. The suffering of the 12 links of dependent origination refers to suffering from the cycle of rebirth expressed as birth to aging-and-death. The consistent explanations of the commentaries are that the forward order of the 12 links of dependent origination reveals the origin of the cycle of rebirth [vaṭṭa] and that the reverse order is the escape from the cycle of rebirth [vivaṭṭa]. (SA.ii.10, etc.)

"The teaching of the 12 links of dependent origination explains the origin and cessation of suffering from the cycle of rebirth. The Buddha said that if one cannot clearly understand the teaching of dependent origination, one cannot escape from the cycle of rebirth."

Dependent Origination: The 12 Links of Dependent Origination and the Twofold Causality Spanning over Three Lifetimes

It is both the Southern Abhidhamma's and the Northern Abhidharma's established theory that the teaching of the 12 links of dependent origination explains the origin and cessation of suffering over three lifetimes.

In the Southern Abhidhamma and the Northern Abhidharma, links 1) ignorance, 2) volitional formations, 8) craving, 9) clinging, and 10) becoming are understood as the two sets of the cause of suffering. Links 3) consciousness, 4) name-and-form, 5) six sense bases, 6) contact, 7) feeling, 11) birth, and 12) aging-and-death are understood as the two sets of effects [suffering]. Because cause and effect repeats twice [cause-effect-cause-effect] over three lifetimes it is called 'the twofold causality spanning over three lifetimes.' This is the established theory of the teaching of dependent origination.

The reason why the 12 links of dependent origination must be seen as an explanation of the cycle of rebirth over three lifetimes is because of links 3) consciousness and 11) birth.

In the Early Buddhist discourses, it is stated, "Ananda, if consciousness were not to come into the mother's womb, would mind and body develop there?" (D15) The commentaries consistently explain that link 3) consciousness of the 12 links of dependent origination is the rebirth-consciousness [paṭisandhiviññāṇa] or the first consciousness of one lifetime. Also, link 11) birth [jāti] is used only when meaning being born into one lifetime.

Therefore, links 1) ignorance, 2) volitional formations are of the past life, 3) consciousness, 4) name-and-form, 5) six sense bases, 6) contact, 7) feeling, 8) craving, 9) clinging, and 10) becoming are of the present life. Links 11) birth and 12) aging-and-death are of the future life. This is the basic starting point of understanding the 12 links of dependent origination.

In other discourses, especially in the *Wise Man and the Fool Discourse* of the Saṃyutta Nikāya (S12:19), dependent origination is explained as occurring over three lifetimes. (Ps.i.51–52; Vis.XVII.288–298) The *Wise Man and the Fool Discourse* is a very important discourse that provides the first clue to this traditional opinion. This discourse interprets the 12 links of dependent origination as 'the twofold causality spanning over three lifetimes,' based on four groups and 20 modes of the 12 links of dependent origination. It is important to notice that the Early Buddhist discourses themselves considered the 12 links of dependent origination as the teaching that highlights the cycle of rebirth over three lifetimes.

The most important fact of the 12 links of dependent origination is that it shows repeated continuation of cause and effect. If this fact is overlooked, the 12 links of dependent origination becomes very confusing.

Let's review this once more: Among the 12 links of dependent origination, links – 1) ignorance, 2) volitional formations, 8) craving, 9) clinging, and 10) becoming – are the links of the cause of suffering; the remaining links – 3) consciousness, 4) name-and-form, 5) six sense bases, 6) contact, 7) feeling, 11) birth, and 12) aging-and-death – are the effect of suffering.

The 12 links of dependent origination show the layered structures of the origin and cessation of suffering through the repeated connections of the links of the cause and effect of suffering.

That said, are ignorance . . . only the cause of the past life and are craving . . . only the cause of the present life? It is not so. In the Path of Purification, these five components are explained: links 1) ignorance, 2) volitional formations, 8) craving, 9) clinging, and 10) becoming can be the causes of past, past life, present, or present life. (Vis.XVII.291) However, ignorance, and volitional formations are more prominent causes for the past life. Craving, clinging, and becoming are more prominent causes for the present life.

When one comes across the 12 links of dependent origination along with various teachings of dependent origination, one must keep in mind the important fact that dependent origination is a powerful method to reveal the non-self. The teaching of dependent origination refuses a supposition of ontological entities such as self, true-self, great-self, master, etc. An attempt to sublimate the teaching of dependent origination as the 'interdependence [paṭṭhāna] of all conditioned phenomena – the 24 modes of conditionality [paccaya]' is to clearly establish the theoretical basis for the non-self of all conditioned phenomena.

In order to eliminate suffering, do all 12 links of dependent origination need to be eliminated? It is not so. Any one of the 12 links can be eliminated. Specifically, if one sees dependent origination as links of cause and effect, the causal links of suffering must be eliminated. The central point of the causal links of suffering is craving. Even the Four Noble Truths list craving as the cause of suffering and the absence of craving as Nibbāna.

Then, how is craving eliminated? One must practice the 37 requisites of enlightenment represented as the noble eightfold path to eliminate craving. The 37 requisites of enlightenment, a detailed method to eliminate suffering and to realize Nibbāna, will be covered in the next chapter.

"The 12 links of dependent origination is the teaching of the origin and cessation of suffering from the cycle of rebirth. It is important to remember that the 12 links of dependent origination is 'the twofold causality spanning over three lifetimes,' wherein the origin and cessation of suffering repeats twice over three lifetimes: past life, present life, and future life."

The Practice of Early Buddhism

ᔥ CHAPTER 6
The 37 Requisites of Enlightenment

What Are the 37 Requisites of Enlightenment?

The purpose of Buddhism is to eliminate suffering and to realize happiness. However, suffering does not disappear by itself. It disappears only when one practices. In the Early Buddhist discourses, 'the practice' refers to the 37 requisites of enlightenment.

The requisites of enlightenment are a direct translation of bodhi pakkhiyā dhamma which means 'Dhamma that are conducive to enlightenment.'

The requisites of enlightenment are classified into seven subjects and are covered in the *Connected Discourses on the Path* [the Maggasaṁyutta Discourse] through the *Connected Discourses on the Bases for Spiritual Power* [the Iddhipādasaṁyutta Discourse] of the Saṁyutta Nikāya.

The requisites of enlightenment, separated into seven subjects, are as follows:

1. The *four* foundations of mindfulness
2. The *four* right efforts

3. The *four* bases for spiritual power
4. The *five* faculties
5. The *five* powers
6. The *seven* factors of enlightenment
7. The noble *eightfold* path

Adding the numbers of the above seven subjects, the sum is 37. Therefore, this is called the 37 requisites of enlightenment. The requisites of enlightenment are explained in the Path of Purification as follows:

> "The fulfilment of states sharing in enlightenment [bodhi] in the fulfilledness of those states partaking [pakkha] in enlightenment. And they 'take the part' of that because they are helpful [upakāra-bhāva]." (Vis.XXII.33)

The term 'requisites of enlightenment' has been translated into Chinese as 助道品, which means 'helpful states,' or 'anything helpful to faith.' Although 助道品 is used more often than the term 'the requisites of enlightenment' in Korea, the Center for Early Buddhist Studies uses the term 'the requisites of enlightenment' since it is the direct translation of the Pāli term.

The commentaries, starting with the Path of Purification, explain that the requisites of enlightenment are on the side of noble ones [the stream-enterer and beyond] who has achieved enlightenment. When one achieves enlightenment, all 37 requisites of enlightenment are present. (Vis.XXII.39) Perhaps, it can only be explained this way because the technical term, the requisites of enlightenment [bodhi pakkhiyā dhamma], literally means 'Dhamma that forms part [pakkhiyā] of enlightenment [bodhi].'

However, from our standpoint as unenlightened beings, certainly, the 37 requisites of enlightenment must be understood as 'Dhamma that is helpful to achieve enlightenment.'

So, the 37 requisites of enlightenment are meaningful and helpful to Buddhists who want to practice! This aspect is absolutely emphasized within the groups of teachings about the 37

requisites of enlightenment in the Saṁyutta Nikāya. (S45-S51)
The Buddha states the following:

> "Bhikkhus, when a bhikkhu does not dwell devoted to development, even though such a wish as this might arise in him:
> 'Oh, that my mind might be liberated from the taints by nonclinging!' yet his mind is not liberated from the taints by nonclinging. For what reason? It should be said: because of nondevelopment. Because of not developing what? Because of not developing the four foundations of mindfulness ...
> the four right efforts ... the four bases for spiritual power ...
> the five faculties ... the five powers ... the seven factors of enlightenment... The noble eightfold path." (S22:101, the Adze Handle [or the Ship] Discourse)

"The practice is outlined in the Early Buddhist discourses as the 37 requisites of enlightenment. The 37 requisites of enlightenment are classified into the following seven subjects: the four foundations of mindfulness, the four right efforts, the four bases for spiritual power, the five faculties, the five powers, the seven factors of enlightenment, and the noble eightfold path."

The Four Foundations of Mindfulness: What is Mindfulness?

The teaching that always appears as the first of the 37 requisites of enlightenment is 'the four foundations of mindfulness [cattāro satipaṭṭhānā].'

Mindfulness is a translation of the Pāli word 'sati' which means 'memory.' However, when sati is used in the Early Buddhist discourses, it never means memory. But when it is attached to anu as in anussati it can mean recollection. The word, saraṇa [remembering] is also used in such context. Of course, when it is used in the context outside of the practice, it may mean memory. In Korea, sati is translated as '마음챙김 [mindfulness].'

In the *Ānāpānasmṛti Discourse*, the second century Buddhist monk, Bhikkhu An Shigao of China transliterated Ānāpāna (in-breath and out-breath) as 安般 [ān-pán] and broadly translated sati not as mind [念] but as a function of defending and protecting the mind [守意].

The following paragraph appears in the *Brahmin Uṇṇābha Discourse* of the Saṁyutta Nikāya.

> "Brahmin, these five faculties take recourse in the mind, and the mind experiences their resort and domain."
> "But, Master Gotama, what is it that the mind takes recourse in?"
> "The mind, brahmin, takes recourse in mindfulness."
> "But, Master Gotama, what is it that mindfulness takes recourse in?"
> "Mindfulness, brahmin, takes recourse in deliverance."
> "But, Master Gotama, what is it that deliverance takes recourse in?"
> "Deliverance, brahmin, takes recourse in Nibbāna."
> "But, Master Gotama, what is it that Nibbāna takes recourse in?"

"You have gone beyond the range of questioning, brahmin. You weren't able to grasp the limit to questioning. For, brahmin, the holy life is lived with Nibbāna as its ground, Nibbāna as its destination, Nibbāna as its final goal." (S48:42, the Brahmin Uṇṇābha Discourse)

Thus, the practice of mindfulness performs an important function of linking the mind to liberation.

In many commentaries, such as in the Path of Purification, five aspects of mindfulness are explained as follows:

1. Mindfulness has the characteristic of penetrating the object.
2. Mindfulness guards the unwholesome dhamma from arising like a door-keeper.
3. Mindfulness grasps the object and discerns it with wisdom.
4. Mindfulness has the characteristic of establishing.
5. Mindfulness protects the mind.

(Vis.XIV.141, XVI.82; DA.iii.758)

The Path of Purification explains, "Strong mindfulness, however, is needed in all instances; for mindfulness protects the mind from lapsing into agitation through faith, energy, and insight, which favour agitation, and from lapsing into idleness through concentration, which favours idleness. So, it is as desirable in all instances as a seasoning of salt in all sauces, as a prime minister in all the king's business." (Vis.IV.49) Thus, mindfulness is beneficial in all instances.

"Mindfulness has the characteristic of penetrating the object.
Mindfulness guards the unwholesome dhamma from arising.
Mindfulness grasps the object.
Mindfulness has the characteristic of establishing.
Mindfulness protects the mind."

The Four Foundations of Mindfulness: The Objects of Mindfulness

Mindfulness is the practice of 'being mindful of an object.' Because there are four objects of mindfulness – body, feeling, mind, and mental objects – it is called establishing four kinds of mindfulness.

In the simile of the six animals in the *Six Animals Discourse* (S35:247) of the Saṃyutta Nikāya, mindfulness is compared to a rope and the object of mindfulness is compared to a post. Here, the six animals represent the six kinds of consciousness. The commentary of the Dīgha Nikāya emphasizes the following:

> "Here, as a trainer of a calf would tie the calf to a post with a rope one must tie one's mind firmly to the object with mindfulness." (DA.iii.763)

Mindfulness [the rope] ties the mind [the calf] to the object [the post]. The practice of mindfulness focuses the mind repeatedly on the object. The foundation of mindfulness is establishing the mind firmly to the selected object. Thus, the most important thing to the mindfulness practice is the object.

The objects of mindfulness are broadly grouped into four categories: body, feeling, mind, and mental objects. In the *Mahāsatipaṭṭāna Discourse* (D22), the four foundations of mindfulness are explained in detail. Also, the objects of mindfulness are further arranged into 21 or 44 types as follows:

BODY [KAYA]: 14 TYPES

1. In-and-out breathing
2. Four kinds of postures
3. Four kinds of clear awareness
4. Reflections on repulsiveness of the 32 body parts
5. Deconstruction of the four great elements

6.–14. Cemetery contemplation

FEELING [VEDANĀ]: NINE TYPES

1. Pleasant feeling
2. Painful feeling
3. Neutral feeling
4. Pleasant feeling with attachment
5. Painful feeling with attachment
6. Neutral feeling with attachment
7. Pleasant feeling without attachment
8. Painful feeling without attachment
9. Neutral feeling without attachment

MIND [CITTA]: 16 TYPES

1. Mind with lust
2. Mind without lust
3. Mind with hatred
4. Mind without hatred
5. Mind with delusion
6. Mind without delusion
7. Contracted mind
8. Distracted mind
9. Developed mind
10. Undeveloped mind
11. Surpassed mind
12. Unsurpassed mind
13. Concentrated mind
14. Unconcentrated mind
15. Liberated mind
16. Unliberated mind

MENTAL OBJECTS [DHAMMA]: FIVE TYPES

1. Observing the hindrances
2. Observing the aggregates

3. Observing the sense bases
4. Observing the factors of enlightenment
5. Observing the truths

The *Mahāsatipaṭṭāna Discourse* clearly shows all objects of mindfulness to be 44 types [or 21 types, when feeling and mind are considered as one object each].

The important point here is that the object of mindfulness is 'I.' The teaching of the five aggregates clearly shows one's impermanence-suffering-non-self by deconstructing 'I' into five aggregates: material form, feeling, perception, mental formations, and consciousness. This is the teaching of the Buddhist theory.

Practicing the four foundations of mindfulness means deconstructing 'I' into 21 or 44 types of body, feeling, mind, or mental objects, picking and being aware of one among these, seeing with insight its impermanence-suffering-non-self, and realizing the revulsion-dispassion-deliverance-knowledge of liberation. This is the teaching of the Buddhist practice.

Therefore, the five aggregates are emphasized first among the six subjects of the Buddhist theory [the five aggregates, the 12 sense bases, the 18 elements, the 22 faculties, the Four Noble Truths, and dependent origination]. The four foundations of mindfulness are emphasized first among the seven subjects of the Buddhist practice [the 37 requisites of enlightenment].

"Mindfulness is 'being mindful of an object.' Because there are four objects of mindfulness [body, feeling, mind, and mental objects], it is referred to as the four foundations of mindfulness."

The Four Foundations of Mindfulness:
Three Similes of Mindfulness

Mindfulness is mainly presented in the discourses using the following three similes.

First, mindfulness is explained using the simile of the rope [rajju] and the post [thambha]. In the *Six Animals Discourse* of the Saṁyutta Nikāya, using the simile of the six animals, mindfulness is compared to the rope and the object of mindfulness is compared to the post. Here, the six animals represent the six kinds of consciousness.

> "Suppose, bhikkhus, a man would catch six animals – with different domains and different feeding grounds – and tie them by a strong rope ... Then those six animals with different domains and different feeding grounds would each pull in the direction of its own feeding ground and domain. ... when these six animals become worn out and fatigued, they would be dominated by the one among them that was strongest; they would submit to it and come under its control.

> "'A strong post or pillar': this, bhikkhus, is a designation for mindfulness directed to the body. Therefore, bhikkhus, you should train yourselves thus: 'We will develop and cultivate mindfulness directed to the body, make it our vehicle, make it our basis, stabilize it, exercise ourselves in it, and fully perfect it.' Thus should you train yourselves." (S35:247, the Simile of the Six Animals Discourse)

Using the foundations of mindfulness, one firmly ties the object of mindfulness to the post using the rope of mindfulness and prevents the mind from favoring the object that arouses unwholesome dhammas.

Second, mindfulness is explained using the simile of the outer door [kavāṭa]. The following stock phrase appears in various places in the Nikāyas about guarding the doors of the six sense faculties [eye, ear, nose, tongue, body, and mind].

> "And how, bhikkhus, is a bhikkhu one who guards the doors of the sense faculties? Here, having seen a visible form with the eye, a bhikkhu does not grasp its signs and features. Since, if he left the eye faculty unrestrained, evil unwholesome states of lust and hatred might invade him, he practices the way of its restraint, he guards the eye faculty, he undertakes the restraint of the eye faculty." (S35:239, the Simile of the Chariot Discourse)

Then, how are the sensory faculties such as the eye faculty restrained? This is explained in the Path of Purification when this stock phrase is unraveled: "He enters upon the way of closing that eye faculty by the door-panel of mindfulness." (Vis.I.56) The door-panel means an outer door, according to dictionaries. For example, when an elegant woman's figure arises at the mind's door, the door-panel of mindfulness of in-and-out breathing must control the sense-door of the mind. Thus, mindfulness is expressed as the door-panel to emphasize the importance of this teaching.

Third, mindfulness is explained using the simile of one's hometown [pettika visaya]. In the *Hawk Discourse* of the Saṁyutta Nikāya, the Buddha compared mindfulness to one's hometown as follows:

> "Bhikkhus, once in the past a hawk suddenly swooped down and seized a quail. Then, while the quail was being carried off by the hawk, he lamented: 'We were so unlucky, of so little merit! We strayed out of our own resort into the domain of others. If we had stayed in our own resort today, in our own ancestral domain, this hawk wouldn't have stood a chance against me in a fight.' – 'But what is your own resort, quail,

what is your own ancestral domain?' – 'The freshly ploughed field covered with clods of soil.'

"Move in your own resort, bhikkhus, in your own ancestral domain. Māra will not gain access to those who move in their own resort, in their own ancestral domain; Māra will not get a hold on them. And what is a bhikkhu's resort, his own ancestral domain? It is the four foundations of mindfulness." (S46:6, the Hawk Discourse)

The above discourse contains the Buddha's sincere words that the way to overcome the mental defilements or Māra (kilesa, ItA.197; ThagA.ii.70) and unwholesome dhammas is to establish mindfulness.

"Mindfulness is compared to
a rope that ties a calf [the mind] to a post [the object],
an outer door that guards the five sensory faculties
[eye, ear, nose, tongue, and body], or
one's hometown that a Buddhist must always rely on."

The Four Foundations of Mindfulness: The Main Focus of Mindfulness Practice

The main points of mindfulness practice are as follows:

First, the object of mindfulness is oneself. It is important to be mindful of the phenomena that are occurring inside of oneself. Those things that occur outside of oneself do not have a great deal of meaning because deliverance·Nibbāna is something one achieves from within.

The *Mahāsatipaṭṭāna Discourse* (D22), among others, said to divide oneself into body, feeling, mind, and mental objects and then further subdivide these into 14, nine, 16, and five types, respectively, or 44 objects in total. Then, select only one of these objects. Of course, he said, one could select an object of mindfulness from another's body, feeling, mind, and mental objects (D22, etc.) using the same method. However, the starting point is always oneself.

Second, most important is deconstruction of conceptual [paññatti] entities. The *Greater Discourse on the Foundations of Mindfulness* (D22) points out the Buddha's reason for deconstructing the objects of mindfulness into body, feeling, mind, and mental objects. The dhamma with the general characteristics of the impermanence·suffering·non-self will appear clearly when conceptual entities such as 'I', mine, mountain, river, computer, automobile, the universe, etc. are deconstructed. Once the impermanence·suffering·non-self of the dhamma are seen, craving and ignorance for those entities should not arise.

Deconstruction is important. The being of 'I' is at the core of deconstruction. Sentient beings presume a true-self and then want to grab onto the unchanging true-self. This is the greatest clinging among all clingings. If something is not deconstructed, one gets fooled by conceptual entities. When one deconstructs and sees the dhamma, then one realizes deliverance·Nibbāna, here and now.

Third, the object is important to mindfulness. The Buddha's suggestion in the *Greater Discourse on the Foundations of Mindfulness* [the Mahāsatipaṭṭāna Discourse] to deconstruct 'I' into body, feeling, mind, and mental objects and to further deconstruct these into 21 or 44 types of mindfulness objects is significant.

If one pursues the question 'Who or what am I?' while 'I' is left as a conceptual being, then one can fall into a false notion of the true self, the genuine self, and the great self; this will lead to inversions of perception as the self being permanent, pleasurable, existing, and attractive [常樂我淨]. However, when 'I' is deconstructed as body, feeling, mind, and mental objects and is seen with insight, impermanence, suffering, non-self, and unattractiveness [無常, 苦, 無我, 不淨] would be deeply felt. As a result, one will realize the revulsion-dispassion-deliverance-knowledge of liberation. (Introduction to Early Buddhism, p. 62)

Fourth, samatha[1] and vipassanā[2] are unified by mindfulness. The practice of Buddhism is largely classified into samatha and vipassanā. Samatha practice is synonymous with the concentration practice and has been translated as 止 [zhǐ] in Chinese. Vipassanā practice is synonymous with the insight practice and has been translated as 觀 [guān] in Chinese. Samatha-vipassanā [zhǐ-guān] is the practice that has sustained Chinese Buddhism.

Without mindfulness, neither concentration nor insight practices are possible. Samatha takes a sign, a conceptual [paññatti] entity, as an object. Vipassanā takes dhamma that arises and perishes moment-to-moment as an object. Regardless of the object, without mindfulness there cannot be samatha that concentrates on a sign nor vipassanā that sees clearly into the impermanence·suffering·non-self of dhamma. Mindfulness, very

---

1 Samatha is concentration meditation practice.
2 Vipassanā is insight meditation practice.

important mental formations, is common to both kinds of practices. Therefore, it is emphasized in the *Fire Discourse*, "But mindfulness, bhikkhus, I say is always useful." (S46:53)

Fifth, it is concluded in the *Connected Discourses on the Foundations of Mindfulness* [the Satipatthāna-Saṁyutta Discourse] and the *Greater Discourse on the Foundations of Mindfulness* [the Mahāsatipaṭṭhāna Discourse] that one must obtain the highest knowledge [aññā] by observing the Four Noble Truths. Among the three characteristics [impermanence·suffering·non-self] of all conditioned phenomena, by clearly knowing the characteristic of the suffering, the origin of suffering, the cessation of suffering, and the way leading to the cessation of suffering, one can realize deliverance·Nibbāna.

According to the Path of Purification, there are three gateways to liberation. These are the impermanence·suffering·non-self.

"When one who has great resolution brings [formations] to mind as impermanent, one acquires the signless liberation. When one who has great tranquility brings [them] to mind as suffering, he acquires the desireless liberation. When one who has great wisdom brings [them] to mind as non-self, he acquires the void liberation." (Vis.XXI.70)

Therefore, the practice of mindfulness concludes in the desireless liberation through insight of suffering. According to Early Buddhist discourses, thoroughly observing the Four Noble Truths is the way to obtain the liberation and the realization of Nibbāna.

"Bhikkhus, these four foundations of mindfulness, when developed and cultivated, lead to utter revulsion, to dispassion, to cessation, to peace, to direct knowledge, to enlightenment, to Nibbāna." (S47:32, the Dispassion Discourse)

"The object of mindfulness is 'I.' Being mindful of phenomena unfolding within 'I' is important because deliverance·Nibbāna is something 'I' achieve from within."

The Four Foundations of Mindfulness: Practicing Mindfulness of In-and-Out Breathing

Among the 21 meditation objects, in-and-out breathing [ānāpāna] is mentioned first. In Chinese, in-and-out breathing has been transliterated as 安般 [ān-pán] and translated as 出入息 [inhalation and exhalation]. In the *Mindfulness of Breathing Discourse* (M118, the Ānāpānasati Discourse) in-and-out breathing appears as an independent subject. The *Connected Discourses on Breathing* (S54, the Ānāpānasaṁyutta Discourse) contains 20 discourses in all. Certainly, in-and-out breathing is a meditation object that deserves special attention.

Through what kind of practice did the Buddha obtain liberation? What method did he, himself, practice? The commentary to the *Greater Discourse to Saccaka* (M36, the Mahāsaccaka Discourse) of the Majjhima Nikāya describes the journey of the Buddha's attainment of liberation. In it, the Buddha concluded that the first jhāna [that he obtained through being 'mindful of in-and-out breathing'] is the way to obtain liberation.

In the *Greater Discourse of Advice to Rāhula* (M62), the Buddha teaches his only son, the Venerable Rāhula this mindfulness practice of in-and-out breathing. Various commentaries mention that the Venerable Ananda and other distinguished direct disciples of the Buddha also obtained the Arahantship through the mindfulness practice of in-and-out breathing. Furthermore, in the commentary of the Dīgha Nikāya, it is explained that all Buddhas, self-enlightened ones [Pacceka-Buddha], and direct disciples of the Buddha enjoy happiness in the present life by establishing mindfulness of in-and-out breathing. (DA.iii.763) Indeed, mindfulness of in-and-out breathing has a very special place within the Buddhist practice.

In the Path of Purification, the indisputable authority of

Theravada Buddhism, mindfulness of in-and-out breathing is explained in detail. In the Path of Purification, the 16-step stock phrase explains the mindfulness practice of in-and-out breathing. (Vis.VIII.145) This stock phrase appears in all discourses of the *Connected Discourses on Breathing* [the Ānāpānasaṃyutta Discourse] as follows:

1. "Breathing in long, he knows: 'I breathe in long'; or breathing out long, he knows: 'I breathe out long.'
2. Breathing in short, he knows: 'I breathe in short'; or breathing out short, he knows: 'I breathe out short.'
3. He trains thus: 'I shall breathe in experiencing the whole body'; he trains thus: 'I shall breathe out experiencing the whole body.'
4. He trains thus: 'I shall breathe in tranquilizing the bodily formations'; he trains thus: 'I shall breathe out tranquilizing the bodily formations.'
5. He trains thus: 'I shall breathe in experiencing happiness'; he trains thus: 'I shall breathe out experiencing happiness.'
6. He trains thus: 'I shall breathe in experiencing bliss'; he trains thus: 'I shall breathe out experiencing bliss.'
7. He trains thus: 'I shall breathe in experiencing the mental formations'; he trains thus: 'I shall breathe out experiencing the mental formations.'
8. He trains thus: 'I shall breathe in tranquilizing the mental formations'; he trains thus: 'I shall breathe out tranquilizing the mental formations.'
9. He trains thus: 'I shall breathe in experiencing the [manner of] consciousness'; he trains thus: 'I shall breathe out experiencing the [manner of] consciousness.'
10. He trains thus: 'I shall breathe in gladdening the [manner of] consciousness'; he trains thus: 'I shall breathe out gladdening the [manner of] consciousness.'
11. He trains thus: 'I shall breathe in concentrating the [manner

of] consciousness'; he trains thus: 'I shall breathe out concentrating the [manner of] consciousness.'

12. He trains thus: 'I shall breathe in liberating the [manner of] consciousness'; he trains thus: 'I shall breathe out liberating the [manner of] consciousness.'

13. He trains thus: 'I shall breathe in contemplating impermanence'; he trains thus: 'I shall breathe out contemplating impermanence.'

14. He trains thus: 'I shall breathe in contemplating fading away'; he trains thus: 'I shall breathe out contemplating fading away.'

15. He trains thus: 'I shall breathe in contemplating cessation'; he trains thus: 'I shall breathe out contemplating cessation.'

16. He trains thus: 'I shall breathe in contemplating relinquishment'; he trains thus: 'I shall breathe out contemplating relinquishment.'"

Of these, 1 through 4 apply to body; 5 through 8 apply to feeling; 9 through 12 apply to consciousness; and 13 through 16 apply to mental objects of the four foundations of mindfulness.

In the Path of Purification, it is explained that "the first tetrad is set forth as a meditation object for a beginner. The other three tetrads are set forth as the contemplation of feeling, of consciousness, and of mental objects, for one who has already attained jhāna." (Vis.VIII.186)

Specifically, in the Path of Purification, this mindfulness practice of in-and-out breathing is explained as "eight stages: 1) counting, 2) connexion, 3) touching, 4) fixing, 5) observing, 6) turning away, 7) purification, and 8) looking back on these." (Vis. VIII.189)

This teaching correlates with the six steps of mindfulness practice as outlined in the *Great Ānāpānasmṛti Discourse* translated by Bhikkhu An Shigao:[3] 1) counting, 2) pursuing, 3) concen-

---

3 Bhikkhu An Shigao [148–180 CE] translated many Indian Buddhist texts into Chinese.

tration, 4) observation, 5) the turning away, and 6) purification. This important teaching is also comparable to the six steps – 1) counting, 2) following, 3) fixing, 4) contemplation, 5) shifting, and 6) purification – and 16 aspects of in-and-out breathing of the *Discourse on the Concentration of Sitting Meditation* (坐禪三昧 經, the Zuochan Sanmei Jing) translated by Bhikkhu Kumurajiva.

In the Path of Purification, mindfulness of in-and-out breathing is explained in detail: "He fixes his mindfulness on the place touched (by the breaths)." (Vis.VIII 194) This is the most important explanation regarding the mindfulness of in-and-out breathing practice. This also is the foundation of the practice taught in various Early Buddhism meditation centers of Myanmar, southeast asia, etc.

"The mindfulness of in-and-out breathing practice has a special place in the Buddhism practice.
The Buddha became enlightened through this practice, many direct disciples of the Buddha attained the Arahantship through this practice. All Buddhas and self-enlightened ones (Pacceka-Buddha)[4] became enlightened through this practice."

---

4 A Pacceka-Buddha attains enlightenment through his own efforts, but does not teach Dhamma to others.

The Four Right Efforts

The 37 requisites of enlightenment encompass the Early Buddhism's practice system, the second subject of which is the four right efforts [cattaro sammappadhāna]. Here, effort [padhāna], striving, or energy [vīriya], have the same meaning. So, what are the four right efforts?

> "Bhikkhus, there are these four right efforts. What four? Here, bhikkhus, a bhikkhu generates desire for the non-arising of unarisen evil unwholesome states;[5] he makes an effort, arouses energy, applies his mind, and strives. He generates desire for the abandoning of arisen evil unwholesome states; he makes an effort, arouses energy, applies his mind, and strives. He generates desire for the arising of unarisen wholesome states; he makes an effort, arouses energy, applies his mind, and strives. He generates desire for the maintenance of arisen wholesome states, for their nondecay, increase, expansion, and fulfillment by development; he makes an effort, arouses energy, applies his mind, and strives." (S49:1, the River Ganges – Eastward, Etc. Discourse)

As shown in this stock phrase, the right efforts or the right strivings consist of four kinds: two kinds for unwholesome dhamma and two kinds for wholesome dhamma. Also these four kinds of right effort are synonymous with the following:

- the right effort [the sixth factor of the noble eightfold path]
- the faculty of energy [the second factor of the five faculties]
- the power of energy [the second factor of the five powers]
- the energy factor of enlightenment [the third factor of the seven factors of enlightenment]

---

5 States refer to dhammas.

· the energy [the second factor of the four bases for spiritual power]

The most important factor of the right effort is distinguishing wholesome dhamma from unwholesome dhamma. Without this, the right effort is not possible. In the seven factors of enlightenment, distinguishing wholesome dhamma from unwholesome dhamma is called the investigation of dhamma factor of enlightenment. Consequently, the investigation of dhamma factor of enlightenment is followed by the energy factor of enlightenment.

In the discourses, the investigation of dhamma factor of enlightenment is defined as follows:

"There are, bhikkhus, wholesome and unwholesome states, blameable and blameless states, inferior and superior states, dark and bright states with their counterparts: frequently giving careful attention to them is the nutriment for the arising of the unarisen enlightenment factor of discrimination of states and for the fulfilment by development of the arisen enlightenment factor of discrimination of states." (S46:2, the Body Discourse)

Then, what are unwholesome dhammas and what are wholesome dhammas? According to the commentaries, unwholesome dhammas are explained as the 14 unwholesome mental factors which overlap with the ten unwholesome actions (DA.ii.644; MA.i.197), the five hindrances (MA.iii.145), etc. The ten unwholesome actions are killing living beings, taking what is not given, sexual misconduct, false speech, malicious speech, harsh speech, gossip, coveting, ill-will, and wrong view. The 14 unwholesome mental factors are delusion, lack of shame, disregard for consequence, restlessness, lust, wrong view, conceit, hatred, envy, miserliness, remorse, sloth, torpor, and doubt.

The wholesome dhammas are explained using the ten wholesome actions and the 37 requisites of enlightenment in the commentaries and in the *Serene Faith Discourse* (D28). The ten whole-some actions are right view and abstaining from the following: killing living beings, taking what is not given, sexual misconduct, false speech, malicious speech, harsh speech, gossip, coveting, and ill-will.

In short, the wholesome dhammas, such as the 37 requisites of enlightenment that brings blameless happy kamma are con-ducive to deliverance·Nibbāna, the ultimate happiness. The ten unwholesome actions and the 14 unwholesome mental factors are the unwholesome dhammas. Accordingly, the right effort or right striving means that one abandons the unwholesome dhammas which hinder deliverance·Nibbāna and arouses the wholesome dhammas which help one realize deliverance·Nibbāna.

"The four right efforts are
to strive for the non-arising of unarisen unwholesome dhammas,
to strive for the abandonment of arisen unwholesome dhammas,
to strive for the arising of unarisen wholesome dhammas,
to strive for the development of arisen wholesome dhammas."

The Four Bases for Spiritual Power

The third subject of the 37 requisites of enlightenment is the four bases for spiritual power [iddhi-pāda]. In the discourses, iddhi means the supernormal power or accomplishment and pāda means foot. In Chinese, this had been translated as 如意足 [the power of ubiquity]. In the commentaries, this is explained in two ways: 'a base for spiritual power' and 'a base which is spiritual power.' (SA.iii.250)

The bases for spiritual power are desire [chanda], energy [viriya], mind [citta], and investigation [vīmaṁsa]. In the discourses, the stock phrase of the four bases for spiritual power appears as follows:

> "Here, bhikkhus, a bhikkhu develops the basis for spiritual power that possesses concentration due to desire and volitional formations of striving. He develops the basis for spiritual power that possesses concentration due to energy and volitional formations of striving. He develops the basis for spiritual power that possesses concentration due to mind and volitional formations of striving. He develops the basis for spiritual power that possesses concentration due to investigation and volitional formations of striving." (S51:1, the From the Near Shore Discourse)

The stock phrase of the bases for spiritual power contains three things: 1) concentration, 2) volitional formations of striving, and 3) four special elements [desire, energy, mind, and investigation] necessary to achieve concentration. As seen here, 'spiritual power' means 'concentration power.' Specifically, through the practice of concentration, 'supernormal power' are obtainable by the fourth jhāna. The four bases for spiritual power are desire, energy, mind, and investigation. These are essential to achieving concentration and supernormal power. In the discourses, the content of the four bases for spiritual power is described as follows:

> "Bhikkhus, if a bhikkhu gains concentration, gains one-pointedness of mind based upon desire, this is called concentration due to desire ... If, bhikkhus, a bhikkhu gains concentration, gains one-pointedness of mind based upon energy ... If, bhikkhus, a bhikkhu gains concentration, gains one-pointedness of mind, based upon mind ... If, bhikkhus, a bhikkhu gains concentration, gains one-pointedness of mind based upon investigation, this is called concentration due to investigation." (S51:13, the Concentration Due to Desire Discourse)

The bases for spiritual power means 'the bases for concentration power' in this teaching.

> "Bhikkhus, whatever samaṇas or brahmins in the past ... Whatever samaṇas or brahmins in the future ... Whatever samaṇas or brahmins at present are of great spiritual power and might, all are so because they have developed and cultivated the four bases for spiritual power." (S51:16, the Samaṇas and Brahmins Discourse)

The bases for spiritual power in this teaching means 'the bases for supernormal power.'

> "Bhikkhus, those who have neglected the four bases for spiritual power have neglected the noble path leading to the complete destruction of suffering. Those who have undertaken the four bases for spiritual power have undertaken the noble path leading to the complete destruction of suffering." (S51:2, the Neglected Discourse)

> "Bhikkhus, these four bases for spiritual power, when developed and cultivated, lead to utter revulsion, to dispassion, to

cessation, to peace, to direct knowledge, to enlightenment, to Nibbāna." (S51:4, the Revulsion Discourse)

The bases for spiritual power in this teaching means 'the bases for enlightenment and Nibbāna.' The comprehensive view of the Early Buddhist discourses is that the four bases for spiritual power can be the bases for concentration, the bases for supernormal power, and the bases for enlightenment and Nibbāna.

"The four bases for spiritual power are
desire, energy, mind, and investigation.
These four are necessary to attain
concentration, supernormal power, and Nibbāna."

The Five Faculties

The fourth subject of the 37 requisites of enlightenment is the five faculties [pañca indriya]. The pañca means five and indriya means faculties or capabilities. In Chinese, this was translated as 五根 [five faculties]. These five faculties are included in the previously reviewed 22 faculties. If the 22 faculties are various faculties organized from a theoretical aspect, the five faculties are a list of capabilities one must practice and develop to realize enlightenment and Nibbāna.

The word Indriya is a derivative of Indra. Indra, a king of gods, appears many times in the Veda literature of India and in the Buddhist literature. It means 'having a directive faculty.' The five faculties [faith, energy, mindfulness, concentration, and wisdom] are listed in the Early Buddhist discourses.

The *Connected Discourses on the Faculties* [the Indriyasaṁyutta Discourse] of the Saṁyutta Nikāya is a collection of teachings relating to the 22 faculties. Excluding the repetitive discourses, 70 discourses are contained in the Indriyasaṁyutta Discourse. Among the 70 discourses, 50 discourses contain the teachings about the five faculties. Clearly, the five faculties are the most important teachings among the 22 faculties.

Various discourses in the *Connected Discourses on the Faculties* emphasize that one becomes a stream-enterer (S48:2), an Arahant (S48:4), etc. by practicing the five faculties (S48:2); one who possesses the five faculties is a true samaṇa and brahmin. (S48:6) Let us take a look at each of the five faculties in detail for its meaning.

"And where, bhikkhus, is the faculty of faith to be seen? The faculty of faith is to be seen here in the four factors of stream-entry.

"And where, bhikkhus, is the faculty of energy to be seen? The faculty of energy is to be seen here in the four right strivings.

"And where, bhikkhus, is the faculty of mindfulness to be seen? The faculty of mindfulness is to be seen here in the four foundations of mindfulness.

"And where, bhikkhus, is the faculty of concentration to be seen? The faculty of concentration is to be seen here in the four jhānas.

"And where, bhikkus, is the faculty of wisdom to be seen? The faculty of wisdom is to be seen here in the Four Noble Truths." (S48:8, the To Be Seen Discourse)

A comprehensive review which compares the above discourses with yet another discourse (S48:10) explains that one must have faith in the Buddha, Dhamma, sangha, and precepts. Energy, here, refers to the four right efforts based on discernment of wholesome dhammas from unwholesome dhammas. Mindfulness, here, refers to being mindful of body, feeling, mind, and mental objects [the four foundations of mindfulness]. Concentration, here, refers to first to fourth jhānas. Wisdom, here, means clearly knowing the Four Noble Truths.

The Path of Purification strongly emphasises the importance of developing the five faculties harmoniously as follows:

"However, what is particularly recommended is balancing faith with wisdom, and concentration with energy. For one strong in faith and weak in wisdom has confidence uncritically and groundlessly. One strong in wisdom and weak in faith errs on the side of cunning and is as hard to cure as one sick of a disease caused by medicine. With the balancing of the two a man has confidence only when there are grounds for it.

"Then idleness overpowers one strong in concentration and weak in energy, since concentration favours idleness. Agitation overpowers one strong in energy and weak in concentration, since energy favors agitation. But concentration coupled with energy cannot lapse into agitation. So these two should be balanced; for absorption comes with the balancing of the two . . .

"Strong mindfulness, however, is needed in all instances; for mindfulness protects the mind from lapsing into agitation through faith, energy and wisdom, which favour agitation, and from lapsing into idleness through concentration, which favours idleness. So it is as desirable in all instances as a seasoning of salt in all sauces, as a prime minister in all the king's business." (Vis.IV.47, 49)

As seen here, faith among the five faculties must be balanced with wisdom; concentration must be balanced with energy; and mindfulness is needed and beneficial in all instances.

"The faculty of faith means having faith in
the Buddha, Dhamma, sangha, and precepts;
the faculty of energy is the four right efforts;
the faculty of mindfulness is being mindful of
body, feeling, mind, and mental objects;
the faculty of concentration is the first through fourth jhāna;
the faculty of wisdom means having a thorough understanding
of the Four Noble Truths."

The Five Powers

The fifth of the seven subjects which make up the 37 requisites of enlightenment is the five powers [pañca-bala]. The five powers is the basic subject of the *Connected Discourses on the Powers* (Balasaṁyutta Discourse) of the Saṁyutta Nikāya. They have the same content as the five faculties and appear in many places within the Early Buddhist discourses. The only difference is that the five powers appear as the power of faith, energy, mindfulness, concentration, and wisdom. (S50:1) The five components (faith, energy, etc.) appear either as faculties or powers. In the Saṁyutta Nikāya, the Buddha said the following:

> "That which is the faculty of faith is the power of faith; that which is the power of faith is the faculty of faith. That which is the faculty of energy is the power of energy; that which is the power of energy is the faculty of energy. That which is the faculty of mindfulness is the power of mindfulness; that which is the power of mindfulness is the faculty of mindfulness. That which is the faculty of concentration is the power of concentration; that which is the power of concentration is the faculty of concentration. That which is the faculty of wisdom is the power of wisdom; that which is the power of wisdom is the faculty of wisdom." (S48:43, the Sāketa Discourse)

According to the Buddha's teaching, there is no basic difference between a faculty and a power. Faculty means control and dominance; power means being unshakable by the opposite. The commentaries explain this further:

> "Because of its perfect control over the characteristic of 'determination,' it is called the 'faculty' of faith; because it is unshakable by the 'opposite faculty,' it is called the 'power' of faith. For the remainders, because of their perfect control over the

characteristics of 'energy,' 'establishment,' 'calmness,' and 'knowledge,' they are called 'faculty'; because they are unshakable by the opposite faculties, – idleness, negligence, agitation, and ignorance – they are called the 'power.'" (SA.iii.247)

To recap, faith, seen from the aspect of determination, becomes the faculty of faith; seen from the aspect of unshakable steadiness from disbelief, it becomes the power of faith. Energy, seen from the aspect of effort, becomes the faculty of energy; seen from the aspect of unshakable steadiness from idleness, it becomes the power of energy.

Mindfulness, seen from the aspect of establishment, becomes the faculty of mindfulness; seen from the aspect of unshakable steadiness from negligence, it becomes the power of mindfulness. Concentration, seen from the aspect of calmness, becomes the faculty of concentration; seen from the aspect of unshakable steadiness from agitation, it becomes the power of concentration. Wisdom, seen from the aspect of knowledge, becomes the faculty of wisdom; seen from the aspect of unshakable steadiness from ignorance, it becomes the power of wisdom. This is the established theory of the Abhidhamma, which differentiates faculty from power.

The Abhidhammattha Sangaha[6] explains, "The faculties are phenomena which exercise control in their respective domains over their associated states ... powers are so called because they cannot be shaken by their opposites and because they strengthen their adjuncts."

"There are no basic differences between faculties and powers, but they can be considered from two different aspects. Faculty means control and power means being unshakable by the opposite."

---

6 A Comprehensive Manual of Abhidhmma

The Five Faculties, The Five Powers, and The Ganhwa-Seon

The *Seonga-gwigam*[7] lists three essential components of the Ganhwa-seon[8] practice: great faith, great energy, and great question. These can be compared to the three legs of a three-legged pot. If these three are not firmly established, hwadu[9] cannot be shattered, gyeonseong[10] is impossible, and the Ganhwa-seon can only be the Uiri-seon.[11]

First, great faith is faith in the hwadu and the teacher who presents it. The *Platform Sutra of the Sixth Patriarch* states, "If one cannot realize one's true nature, then by all means, see one's true nature through teaching from a realiable teacher of Buddhism." Bhikkhu Dahui[12] said, "If there is this mind [faith], there wouldn't be anyone who cannot become a Buddha. Although the lay practitioners learn Dhamma, they create stumbling blocks by themselves due to lack of firm faith." The great faith corresponds to the first of the five faculties.

---

7 *Seonga-gwigam* [선가귀감] or the *Mirror of the Seon School* is a collection of teachings and aphorisms from classical seon and pre-seon literature offering instruction on seon practice, along with commentary by Bhikkhu Hyujeong [휴정, 1520–1604]

8 Ganhwa-seon is the phrase-observing meditation or gong-an contemplation. A seon meditation method seeks direct attainment of enlightenment through investigation of the 'key phrase' [hwadu, 화두, 話頭].

9 Hwadu is also known as the great question, doubt, or gong-an and used in the Ganhwa-seon which is the principal type of meditation practiced in contemporary Korean Buddhism.

10 Gyeonseong [seeing the Buddha nature or one's own originally enlightened mind] is a common saying of the Seon school.

11 Uiri-seon [theoretical seon] is seon practiced according to the doctrinal principles of the discourses.

12 Bhikkhu Dahui [1089–1163] was a master of the Seon [Chan or Zen] school of the Southern Song dynasty of China.

Second, great energy refers to an incessant and progressive practice of penetrating the hwadu. It can be described as the continuous effort of being mindful of the hwadu and not being controlled by idleness or other unwholesome dhammas.

It requires one to make a sincere effort and not back down while focusing on the hwadu, even risking one's life to do so! This great energy is the second element of the five faculties.

Third, great question refers to the state of 'the ball of doubt shining independently (疑團獨露, 의단독로)' in which one can go neither forward nor backward due to great doubt about the hwadu. Bhikkhu Dahui, the pioneer of the Ganhwa-seon pointed out that unless one overcomes the seon sicknesses of torpor, remorse, restlessness, mental proliferation, etc. one cannot escape from the seduction of the cycle of rebirth.

One of the basic reasons why Bhikkhu Dahui advocated the Ganhwa-seon is that the focus necessary to penetrate the hwadu is the most powerful means to rid oneself of torpor and restlessness. Here, torpor is overcome by repeatedly focusing on the hwadu. Focusing on the hwadu equates with the faculty of wisdom of the five faculties. Restlessness is overcome by closely concentrating on the hwadu; this meticulous attention is the faculty of concentration of the five faculties. We call this meticulous attention of the hwadu 'being mindful of the hwadu.' Here, being mindful means that the mind has a watertight focus on the hwadu; this is the faculty of mindfulness of the five faculties.

There are five essential components in the study of hwadu: 1) innately pure mind and faith in a reliable Buddhist teacher, 2) energy, 3) mindfulness of the hwadu, 4) calm abiding, and 5) wisdom that transcends the sphere of cognition. As seen here, great faith, great energy, and great question of the Ganhwa-seon have the same content of Early Buddhism's five faculties or the five powers: faith, energy, mindfulness, concentration, and wisdom. Indeed, great question of the Ganhwa-seon can be explained as the heightened state of three mental formations [mindfulness, concentration, and wisdom] of Early Buddhism and Theravada Buddhism.

Since the Ganhwa-seon is also a Buddhist practice, its theoretical basis must be found in the Buddha's teaching. Especially, how to understand or interpret the arousing of the great question [the most emphasized component in the Ganhwa-seon] within the framework of the Buddhist theory, is a very important matter. I think a viewpoint that explains great question as a harmonious development of mindfulness, concentration, and wisdom – the core of Early Buddhism's practice methods – will definitely be evaluated in the future.

"Great faith, great energy, and great question of the Ganhwa-seon have the same content as the five faculties or the five powers of Early Buddhism: faith, energy, mindfulness, concentration, and wisdom."

The Seven Factors of Enlightenment

The seven factors of enlightenment [satta bojjhaṅga] is the sixth of the seven subjects of the 37 requisites of enlightenment. It is also the subject of the *Connected Discourses on the Factors of Enlightenment* [the Bojjhaṅgasaṁyutta Discourse] of the Saṁyutta Nikāya.

Here, bojjhaṅga is translated as 'the factors of enlightenment' and is a compound word made up of enlightenment [bodhi] and factor [aṅga]. The commentaries explain this compound word in two ways, as 'the factors of enlightenment' or 'the factors of the enlightened one.' In the discourses, the meaning mostly appears as the former. The seven factors of enlightenment are categorized as follows:

1. The mindfulness factor of enlightenment [sati-sambojjhaṅga]
2. The investigation of dhamma factor of enlightenment [dhamma-vicaya-sambojjhaṅga]
3. The energy factor of enlightenment [vīriya-sambojjhaṅga]
4. The rapture factor of enlightenment [pīti-sambojjhaṅga]
5. The tranquility factor of enlightenment [passaddhi-sambojjhaṅga]
6. The concentration factor of enlightenment [samādhi-sambojjhaṅga]
7. The equanimity factor of enlightenment [upekkhā-sambojjhaṅga]

In the Early Buddhist discourses, the seven factors of enlightenment always appear in this particular order.

1. One must become mindful of any one of the 21 or 44 mindfulness objects.
2. One must investigate whether it is wholesome dhamma that leads to deliverance·Nibbāna or not.

3. One must strive to increase wholesome dhammas and abandon unwholesome dhammas.
4. One experiences rapture.
5. One's mind experiences tranquility.
6. One's mind achieves absorption concentration.
7. One's mind attains equanimity and is free and unshakable from all conditioned phenomena.

This is the basic teaching of the seven factors of enlightenment presented to practitioners.

Then why did the Buddha explain only these seven as the factors of enlightenment? Stated in the commentaries, the Buddha explained them in this manner that is neither short nor excessive, 'because these seven factors are useful everywhere and are the opposites of torpor and restlessness.' According to the commentaries, the Buddha explained that for the state of torpor, it is appropriate to practice three factors of enlightenment [investigation, energy, and rapture], the opposites of torpor; for the state of restlessness, it is appropriate to practice three factors of enlightenment [tranquility, concentration, and equanimity], the opposites of restlessness; and the mindfulness factor of enlightenment is useful everywhere. (MA.i.85)

In the discourses, the seven factors of enlightenment appear as the opposite of the five hindrances. For example, as stated in the *Obstructions Discourse*, the characteristics of the five hindrances are "obstructions, hindrances, corruptions of the mind, and weakeners of wisdom." However, the characteristics of the seven factors of enlightenment are "nonobstructions, nonhindrances, noncorruptions of the mind; when developed and cultivated, they lead to the realization of the fruit of true knowledge and liberation." (S46:37)

Meanwhile, the discourses, the Abhidhamma, and the commentaries each shows different positions on the seven factors of enlightenment. The discourses refer to the seven factors of enlightenment as 'the mundane paths' for the unenlightened ones. They emphasize the need to practice the seven factors of enlightenment to achieve enlightenment. (S46:5) The Abhidhamma states that these seven factors are 'the supramundane paths' for the stream-enterer to the Arahant, the enlightened noble ones, to complete and obtain. (Vbh.229–232) The commentary literature explains that the seven factors of enlightenment applies to both the mundane and the supramundane paths – 'a mixed path.' (SA.iii.138)

"One must become mindful of an object among the mindfulness objects; one must investigate whether it is wholesome dhamma that leads to deliverance-Nibbāna or not; one must strive to increase wholesome dhammas and abandon unwholesome dhammas. By practicing so, one experiences rapture and one's mind experiences tranquility. One's mind achieves the absorption concentration and obtains equanimity, free and unshakable from all conditioned phenomena.**"**

The Noble Eightfold Path: The First and the Last Discourses of the Buddha

The noble eightfold path is the seventh or the last of the 37 requisites of enlightenment. Literally, in Korean and Chinese, 팔정도, 八正道 means eight 'right' paths. In the discourses, it always appears as 'the noble path with eight components [ariya aṭṭhaṅgika magga].'

Then, why was this called the eight 'right' paths in Korea instead of 'noble' paths. The reason can be found in the *Four Āgama Discourses* [Chinese translation]. It is almost always translated as the eight 'right' paths in the Chinese translation of various discourses including the *Mādhyamâgama*, the *Saṃyuktâgama*, and the *Ekôttarâgama* of the *Four Āgama Discourses*. As a result, it is firmly established to be the eight 'right' paths in Korea. It seems that because of the emphasis on the word 'right' from the right view to the right concentration, it may have been translated as the eight 'right' paths. The noble eightfold path is also the subject of the *Maggasaṃyutta* of the Saṃyutta Nikāya.

The noble eightfold path is the first and the last discourses of the Buddha. The *Setting in Motion the Wheel of the Dhamma Discourse* which contains the Buddha's first discourse emphasizes this as follows:

> "Bhikkhus, these two extremes should not be followed by one who has gone forth into homelessness. What two? The pursuit of sensual happiness in sensual pleasures, which is low, vulgar, the way of worldlings, ignoble, unbeneficial; and the pursuit of self-mortification, which is painful, ignoble, unbeneficial. Without veering towards either of these extremes, the Tathāgata has awakened to the middle path, which gives rise to vision, which gives rise to knowledge, which leads to peace, to direct knowledge, to enlightenment, to Nibbāna.

"And what, bhikkhus, is that middle path awakened to by the Tathāgata, which gives rise to vision ... which leads to Nibbāna? It is this noble eightfold path; that is, right view, right intention, right speech, right action, right livelihood, right effort, right mindfulness, and right concentration." (S56:11, the Setting in Motion the Wheel of the Dhamma Discourse)

The *Great Passing Discourse* (D16, Mahāparinibbāna Discourse) contains the records of the Buddha's last days. According to this discourse, prior to giving his last five dying instructions, the Buddha gave his last teachings to the wonderer Subbadha in discourse format.

Subbadha asked the Buddha if the six non-Buddhist masters have realized the truth. The Buddha replied as follows:

"In whatever Dhamma and discipline the noble eightfold path is not found, no samana is found, no samana is found of the first, the second, the third, or the fourth grade. But such samanas can be found, of the first, second, third, and fourth grade in a Dhamma and discipline where the noble eightfold path is found. Now Subbadha, in this Dhamma and discipline the noble eightfold path is found, and in it are to be found samanas of the first, second, third, and fourth grade." (D16, The Great Passing Discourse)

Here, the commentaries explain, "the first samana is the stream-enterer, the second samana is the once-returner, the third samana is the non-returner, and the fourth samana is the Arahant." (MA.ii.4–5)

Just before the Buddha's passing, he taught Subbadha that, "[where] the noble eightfold path is found ... in it are to be found samanas." This is the great lion's roar which has lasted throughout all generations of Buddhism. The Buddha started his first discourse with the middle path, the noble eightfold path, and he finished his last discourse with the middle path, the noble eightfold path.

As seen in the *Great Steward Discourse* [the Mahāgovinda Discourse], when the Buddha was Mahāgovinda in his previous life, because he did not know the noble eightfold path and he could not realize Nibbāna, he could merely be reborn in the Bramā world. However, because he realized Nibbāna through the practice of the noble eightfold path in this life, he is sharing his knowledge of the path so that others might overcome the cycle of rebirth and attain Nibbāna.

> "Pañcasikha ... my holy life leads unfailingly to disenchantment, to dispassion, to cessation, to peace, to direct knowledge, to enlightenment, to Nibbāna. That is the noble eightfold path, namely right view, right intention, right speech, right action, right livelihood, right effort, right mindfulness, and right concentration." (D19, the Great Steward Discourse)

In addition, the *About Mahāli Discourse* (D6), the *Great Lion's Roar Discourse* (D8), the *About Payasi Discourse* (D23), etc., state that the noble eightfold path is the most remarkable teaching and is only taught in Buddhism.

"The noble eightfold path is the teaching that shows the path to Nibbāna. The Buddha began his first discourse with the noble eightfold path [the middle path] and finished his last discourse with the noble eightfold path."

The Noble Eightfold Path: The Eight Components

Let's examine each component of the noble eightfold path based on explanations given in the discourses and commentaries.

First, the right view [sammā-diṭṭhi] is defined as, "knowledge of suffering, knowledge of the origin of suffering, knowledge of the cessation of suffering, knowledge of the way leading to the cessation of suffering" in the *Analysis Discourse*. (S45:8) In other words, the right view is knowledge of the Four Noble Truths.

The *Kaccānagotta Discourse* emphasizes that the teaching of dependent origination is the right view. The Buddha clearly said, "'All exists': Kaccāna, this is one extreme. 'All does not exist': this is the second extreme. Without veering towards either of these extremes, the Tathāgata teaches the Dhamma by the middle." (S12:15) He expounded 'the middle' with this stock phrase – the forward and reverse orders of the 12 links of dependent origination.

The right view is knowledge of the Four Noble Truths and the teaching of dependent origination. By the way, the noble truth of suffering and the noble truth of the origin of suffering of the Four Noble Truths are connected to the forward order of dependent origination; the noble truth of the cessation of suffering and the noble truth of the way leading to the cessation of suffering are connected to the reverse order of dependent origination.

Therefore, the Four Noble Truths and the teaching of dependent origination have the same content. This is the correct understanding of the right view of the noble eightfold path.

The Venerable Sāriputta states clearly that the right view is thoroughly knowing the following four points in the *Right View Discourse* (M9):

1. The wholesome and the unwholesome
2. The four kinds of nutriment, the origin of nutriment, the

cessation of nutriment, the way leading to the cessation of
nutriment
3. The Four Noble Truths
4. The 12 links of dependent origination

Second, the right intention [sammā-saṅkappa] is defined as,
"intention of renunciation, intention of non-ill will, intention
of harmlessness." (S45:8) The right intention can adamantly be
expressed as possessing the four sublime abidings [cattāro brah-
mavihāra] that the Buddha emphasized in the Early Buddhist
discourses: loving-kindness, compassion, sympathetic joy, and
equanimity.

Third, the right speech [sammā-vācā] is defined as, "abstinence
from false speech, abstinence from divisive speech, abstinence
from harsh speech, and abstinence from idle chatter." (S45:8)

Fourth, the right action [sammā-kammanta] is, "abstinence
from the destruction of life, abstinence from taking what is not
given, abstinence from sexual misconduct." (S45:8) The abstinence from sexual misconduct is the rule for the lay Buddhists
(D31) and abstinence from all sexual conduct is the rule for the
bhikkhus and bhikkunis. (D2)

Fifth, the right livelihood [sammā-ājīva] is about one who,
"having abandoned a wrong mode of livelihood, earns his living
by a right livelihood." (S45:8) The monastics must make a living
receiving alms and observing non-possession. Very importantly
monastics should not engage in fortune-telling and divination.
(D2) Lay Buddhists must make a living by engaging in a proper
occupation or trade. The *Trades Discourse* (A5:177) lists five trades
lay Buddhists should not be engaged in: trading in weapons, trading in living beings, trading in meat, trading in intoxicants, and
trading in poisons.

Sixth, the right effort [sammā-vāyāma] is, "generating desire
for nonarising of unarisen evil unwholesome states; he makes an
effort, arouses energy, applies his mind, and strives. He generates

desire for the abandoning of arisen evil unwholesome states ... He generates desire for the arising of unarisen wholesome states ... He generates desire for the maintenance of arisen wholesome states, for their non-decay, increase, expansion, and fulfilment by development; he makes an effort, arouses energy, applies his mind, and strives." (S45:8) Therefore, discerning the wholesome dhamma that leads to deliverance·Nibbāna from unwholesome dhamma precedes the right effort.

Seventh, the right mindfulness [sammā-sati] is, "dwelling, contemplating the body in the body ... contemplating feelings in feelings ... contemplating mind in mind ... contemplating mental objects in mental objects ... One must be ardent, clearly comprehending and mindful, having removed lust and hatred in regard to the world." (S45:8) The right mindfulness is the concrete practice technique presented by the noble eightfold path. The Buddha expounds further, saying one must deconstruct the being, 'I' as body, feeling, mind, and mental objects, focus on one of these objects, and know and see clearly the impermanence·suffering·non-self.

Eighth, the right concentration [sammā-samādhi] means, entering and dwelling in the first, second, third, and fourth jhāna. (S45:8) Having overcome the five hindrances [sensual desire, ill will, sloth and torpor, restlessness and remorse, and doubt] and by practicing the right concentration, one attains the four jhānas, progressively experiencing the rapture-happiness-tranquility-equanimity.

"The noble eightfold path is a noble path with eight components: right view, right intention, right speech, right action, right livelihood, right effort, right mindfulness, and right concentration."

The Noble Eightfold Path: The Noble Eightfold Path is the Middle Path

As seen in the Buddha's first discourse, the *Setting in Motion the Wheel of the Dhamma Discourse* (S56:11), the middle path is the noble eightfold path. Except for the *Naked Samaṇa Kassapa Discourse*, (S12:17) (A3:151–152) which shows the entire 37 requisites of enlightenment as the middle path, all other Early Buddhist discourses explain that the middle path is the noble eightfold path. The 'middle' referred to in the *Eight Negations of the Middle Way* or the *Emptiness, Nominal Existence, and the Middle* of the Mādhyamaka-sāstra[13] is not called the middle path in the Early Buddhist discourses.

Some confusion regarding the middle path stems from the Mādhyamaka-sāstra of Mahāyāna Buddhism. The Mādhyamaka-sāstra insists that the 'middle' of the *Emptiness, Nominal Existence, and the Middle* is the middle path. But the 'middle' here does not simply mean the median but means avoiding the two extremes of existence and non-existence. It is explained in the Mādhyamaka-sāstra that emptiness is due to dependent origination and therefore the 'middle' is the middle path. Also, the middle path is used as a technical term to explain – avoiding neither one nor many, neither coming nor going, neither existent nor non-existent, and neither eternal nor impermanent.

However, according to the *Kaccānagotta Discourse* (S12:15) which is the basis of Bhikkhu Nargajuna's theory, the Buddha stressed the importance of not seeing this world with an extreme view – this world 'exists [atthi] or does not exist [natthi]' – but to see this world as being governed by dependent origination of 'arising [samudaya] and cessation [nirodha].' As seen in this dis-

---

13 The Mādhyamaka-sāstra [Jungnon] is the basic teaching of the Mādhyamaka School.

course, Tathāgata teaches the Dhamma 'by the middle' [majjha], without veering towards either extreme of 'exists or does not exist.' The important point here is that one must avoid the 'exist or does not exist' mentality. This is the 'middle' and is certainly not stated as the middle path.

Further, the *Threefold Truth* of the Mādhyamaka-sāstra explains that clearly seeing the *Emptiness, Nominal Existence, and the Middle* of dependently originated phenomena is the middle path. This middle path mentioned in the Mādhyamaka-sāstra is seeing dependent origination with insight. Therefore, this middle path refers to the first component of the noble eightfold path, the right view. This does not refer to the practice of the noble eightfold path.

By comparison, the middle path of the Early Buddhist discourses refers to the practice and does not refer to philosophy or view. One takes a big risk in making the middle path a theoretical exercise rather than accepting it as the practice. The fact that the 'middle' refers to dependent origination and the middle path refers to none other than the noble eightfold path cannot be forgotten. When the word practice [paṭipadā, paṭipatti] is added to the word middle [majjha, majjhima], it becomes the middle path [majjhima-paṭipatti].

Stated in another way, the middle path is practicing the eight kinds of right path [right view, right intention, right speech, right action, right livelihood, right effort, right mindfulness, and right concentration], or right practice based on the insight of dependent origination. As emphasized in many places within the Early Buddhist discourses, this practice is about being devoted to the here and now [diṭṭhe va dhamme]. The middle path is knowing and seeing the reality [yathā-bhūta-ñāṇa-dassana] of dependent origination here and now and practicing righteousness each and every moment.

It is wonderful that more and more people recognize that the middle path is the noble eightfold path as Early Buddhism rapidly takes root in Korea. Early Buddhism is the root of Buddhism. Now, I would like to emphasize that the middle path that the Buddha sincerely spoke of must be understood as the practice of the noble eightfold path. It must not be dismissed as a mere opinion or philosophy of the neither existent nor non-existent, the neither suffering nor pleasure, the *Eight Negations of the Middle Way*, etc.

"The middle path presented by the Early Buddhist discourses is the noble eightfold path.
The 'middle' refers to dependent origination and corresponds to the right view of the noble eightfold path.
The 'middle path' refers to practicing the eight kinds of right path based on the insight of dependent origination."

The Noble Eightfold Path: The Core Teaching of the Noble Eightfold Path

The important points of the noble eightfold path are as follows:

First, once again the noble eightfold path is the middle path. For those Koreans who are familiar with Mahāyāna Buddhism, the first thing they may think of when they hear the middle path is the *Eight Negations of the Middle Way* or the *Threefold Truth* of the Mādhyamaka-sāstra. However, in the Early Buddhist discourses, the middle path is clearly the noble eightfold path.

The *Eight Negations of the Middle Way* are defined as avoiding neither one nor many, neither coming nor going, neither existent nor non-existent, and neither eternal nor impermanent. The *Threefold Truth* of the Mādhyamaka-sāstra is defined as the *Emptiness, Nominal Existence, and the Middle.*

Second, the noble eightfold path or the middle path is not a philosophy but a system of practice. Some like to explain in various ways the meanings of the 'middle' based on philosophical intentions. Unfortunately, those explanations may risk turning the middle path, a system of practice, into a theoretical exercise. The Buddha defined the middle path in the stock phrase of the noble eightfold path. The middle path is practicing this teaching of the Buddha. This can also be seen in the Pāli word, paṭipadā which means actually stepping on the path [paṭi] while walking [padā]. The paṭipadā means walking the path – the middle path.

Third, the practice of the noble eightfold path is a comprehensive practice. Yet, we do not try to understand and practice it in a comprehensive manner. Instead, we only try to understand the practice as a technique. Therefore, we insist that only a certain practice such as seon [chan or zen], mantra, prayer, or vipassanā is a true practice, and we veer toward the extremes. However, the Buddha did not say only certain technique or one special kind of practice is the path. Instead, he said eight kinds or the noble eightfold path is the path. When these eight kinds are developed harmoniously in a comprehensive manner, that is the right path or the middle path.

Fourth, the noble eightfold path is right here and now. The practice does not exist only in a special place or time. It does not exist only when one meditates, chants, prays, or prostrates. It does not exist only at a specific place, like a Buddhist temple, meditation room, or retreat center. That is why Bhikkhu Linji Yixuan said, "Only right here and now exists, no other good season exists." The noble eightfold path must be practiced right here and now.

Fifth, the noble eightfold path cannot be done in one fell swoop. The Buddha said sincerely and emphasized repeatedly in the Early Buddhist discourses that practicing the noble eightfold path means to practice and to study a lot. This is emphasized in many places in the *Connected Discourses on the Path* (S45). Taking the middle path means that one should practice the noble eightfold path repeatedly. The unenlightened ones practice the noble eightfold path, the middle path, to realize liberation. The enlightened ones are the embodiment of liberation on this earth because of their practice of the noble eightfold path.

The commentaries explain the former [the unenlightened ones] as being on the 'preparatory path.' Both the former and the latter [the enlightened ones] are on the 'mixed path.' (DA.ii.301) Nibbāna is preceded by the preparatory path. The mixed path is a combination of preparatory path and Nibbāna.

Buddha's teaching has been called the Buddha's command since the time of the Buddha's direct disciples. The Buddha's command is the practice of the middle path, the noble eightfold path, void of extremes. We must take to heart the Buddha's stern command to 'realize deliverance-Nibbāna, right here and now by practicing the noble eightfold path.'

"The Buddha did not say a certain technique or special one thing is the path. Instead he spoke of the eight kinds of path, the noble eightfold path. When these eight are developed harmoniously in a comprehensive manner, that is the right path, the middle path."

❧ CHAPTER 7
Samatha and Vipassanā

Samatha and Vipassanā: the Buddha's Direct Teaching

Samatha and vipassanā are the representative technical terms of the Buddhist practice. They are the core technical terms that illustrate most clearly the practice system of Theravada Buddhism. Early on, these two technical terms were translated as 止 [concentration] and 觀 [seeing] in Chinese.

The important literary works of Bhikkhu Yeongga Hyeongak [永嘉玄覺], a direct disciple of the Sixth Patriarch Venerable Huineng [慧能] and also the famous author of *Jeungdo Ga* [Song of Actualizing the Way], include *Seonjong Yeongga Jip* [禪宗永嘉集]. This book has ten chapters in all. The core of the practice section is three chapters: chapter four, titled Samatha; chapter five, titled Vipassanā; and chapter six, titled Upekkhā[1].

Therefore, we know that samatha and vipassanā were deeply understood in China early on. It has been taught that these practices – concentration [samatha] and insight [vipassanā] – should

---

1 Upekkhā means equanimity.

be done in tandem. This practice has been translated as 止觀兼修 [practicing samatha and vipassanā together]. In Seon Jong[2] [Chan Zong or Zen], it has come to be understood as 定慧雙修 [practicing samatha and vipassanā together] through the generations.

Then, this begs the question, did the Buddha personally expound on samatha and vipassanā in the Early Buddhist discourses? How did the Buddha define samatha and vipassanā?

The Buddha clearly defines samatha and vipassanā in many of the Early Buddhist discourses. In the *Fools Discourse* (A2:3:11) of the Aṅguttara Nikāya, the Buddha definitely connects samatha with concentration [samadhi] and vipassanā with insight [paññā]. He clarifies that concentration is a practice one uses to overcome desire and insight is a practice one uses to overcome ignorance.

The *Concentration Discourse* of the Aṅguttara Nikāya supplies clear answers regarding samatha and vipassanā. The expressions of 'internal serenity of mind' and 'higher wisdom of insight,' are seen in these three discourses (A4:92–94). Samatha is a practice of developing serenity or having serenity. Vipassanā is a practice of developing insight or having insight.

The *Concentration Discourse* explains that in order to obtain samatha, one can approach another who gained internal serenity of mind and inquire, "How, friend, should the mind be steadied? How should the mind be composed? How should the mind be unified? How should the mind be concentrated?" (A4:94)

The Buddha explains that in order to obtain vipassanā, one can approach another who gained the higher wisdom of insight into conditioned phenomena and inquire, "How, friend, should conditioned phenomena be seen? How should conditioned phenomena be explored? How should conditioned phenomena be discerned by insight?" (A4:94)

The Buddha had clearly shown samatha is a practice to develop concentration by fixing the mind on an object and

---

2 Seon Jong is a representative order of Korean Buddhism.

achieving serenity; vipassanā is a practice to contemplate and observe conditioned phenomena [saṇkhāra] allowing one to clearly see the impermanence·suffering·non-self of conditioned phenomena.

The commentary literature describes samatha and vipassanā separately as mundane samatha [lokiya-samatha], supramundane samatha [lokuttara-samatha], mundane vipassanā [lokiya-vipassanā], and supramundane vipassanā [lokuttara-vipassanā]. (SA.iii.121; Pm.15; MAT.i.238, etc.) Concentration and insight are also described separately as mundane concentration, supramundane concentration, mundane insight, and supramundane insight. (DA.ii.425; UdA.69, etc.) The supramundane [lokuttara] takes Nibbāna as its meditation object (Vis.XIV.15, etc.). The mundane [lokiya] does not take Nibbāna as its meditation object.

For those who have not experienced the path and the fruit, I would like to clarify the fact that samatha and vipassanā discussed in this entire book is about the practice of mundane samatha and mundane vipassanā – the practice to experience the path and the fruit and to realize Nibbāna. The supramundane samatha and vipassanā are not included here. The mundane samatha and vipassanā – the practice of experiencing the path and fruit and realizing Nibbāna – are meaningful and relevant to us. Also, the explanations including the supramundane can make samatha and vipassanā a controversial debate at the slightest slip of interpretation.

"In the Early Buddhist discourses, the Buddha clearly defined samatha and vipassanā. Samatha is a practice of developing concentration to bring serenity of mind. Vipassanā is a practice of exploring conditioned phenomena to clearly see the impermanence·suffering·non-self with insight."

Samatha and Vipassanā:
Comparison of Samatha and Vipassanā

Examining samatha and vipassanā by comparison from several perspectives shows the following:

First, in both samatha or vipassanā, it is imperative to establish the meditation object clearly. Seeing from the mundane state, the object of samatha is a sign [nimitta][3], a concept [paññatti]. The object of vipassanā is phenomena [dhamma]. This is the most important measuring stick to distinguish samatha from vipassanā.

Second, samatha is a practice of developing concentration by focusing on an object – a sign. Vipassanā is a practice of seeing, with insight, the impermanence·suffering·non-self of the conditioned phenomena. Samatha is the serene state of mind achieved by concentrating the mind on a sign and steadying tremors and disturbances of the mind. Therefore, in Chinese, it is translated as 止 [concentration]. With vipassanā, one does not see the object from a conventional mode but sees the impermanence·suffering·non-self, the characteristics of dhamma, with insight, in accordance with vipassanā's literal meaning of 'deconstruct [vi] and see [passanā].' Therefore, in Chinese, it is translated as 觀 [seeing].

Third, the key word for samatha is a sign and the key words for vipassanā are the impermanence·suffering·non-self. In the Path of Purification, there are 40 meditation objects of concentration. If one takes a narrow definition of the samatha practice as a practice to obtain absorption-concentration (M.A.ii.346), samatha is about taking one object among the 22 meditation objects of the 40 meditation objects, then one concentrates the mind on it and creates a learning sign [uggaha-nimitta] from the object.

---

3 Nimittas refer to signs or images.

Eventually this learning sign is purified into a counterpart sign [patibhāga-nimitta] that does not scatter and becomes whole. At this point, the mind is extremely focused on this counterpart sign each and every moment. Vipassanā is a practice of seeing with insight one of the 71 ultimate realities that are further classified as mind, mental factors, and materiality. In this way, when one sees the dhamma with insight, the impermanence·suffering·non-self can be clearly seen.

Fourth, there are different kinds of concentration: the concentration attained through samatha is access-concentration [upacāra-samādhi] or absorption-concentration [appanā-samādhi]; intense concentration attained during vipassanā practice is momentary-concentration [khanika-samādhi].

Fifth, deliverance·Nibbāna cannot be realized through the serenity of samatha only. Because samatha is a state in which the mind and the meditation object become one, the lust·hatred·delusion are suppressed and lie dormant by clear and bright serenity. However, once one is out of samatha, the lust·hatred·delusion's influence returns. This state is called 'temporarily liberated' [samaya-vimutta] in the discourses. (A5:149) Therefore, the lust·hatred·delusion must be eradicated through the power of vipassanā that clearly sees the impermanence·suffering·non-self with insight. As a result, those taints will not arise again and deliverance·Nibbāna can be realized.

Without the wisdom of vipassanā, deliverance is impossible. However, it is definitely not easy to obtain the wisdom of vipassanā without the aid of samatha. Therefore, in the Early Buddhist discourses, the technical terms like samatha and vipassanā almost always appear together. The Buddha emphasized practicing these two diligently.

Sixth, whether one should practice samatha first, vipassanā first, or practice both simultaneously is ultimately up to one's teacher or one's own interest and preference. In the *In Conjunction Discourse*, the Buddha said all states from first jhāna to 'cessation of perception and feeling' become firm bases for the attainment of Arahantship. (A4:170) Of course, one who practices dry vipassanā [sukkah-vipassaka], in other words, pure vipassanā [suddha-vipassaka] can only obtain the Arahantship by practicing the dry vipassanā without the moisture of jhāna.[4] (DA.i.4)

In conclusion, one may practice samatha first, vipassanā first, or samatha and vipassanā simultaneously. Saying that one must practice samatha first or vipassanā first is a mere dogmatic opinion; one cannot be called a true practitioner while insisting so. In any circumstances, the important matter is that the Buddhist practice always ends up in vipassanā, insight of the impermanence-suffering-non-self. Vipassanā mentioned here is seeing clearly the impermanence-suffering-non-self and does not refer to any specific practice method.

"Samatha is a practice in which one focuses on an object called a sign and develops concentration. Vipassanā is a practice in which one sees clearly the impermanence-suffering-non-self of dhamma and develops insight.**"**

---

4 The 'moisture of jhāna' means the rapture and happiness of jhāna.

Samatha and Vipassanā: Absorption-Concentration and Momentary Concentration

The Buddha explained that concentration is 'one-pointedness of mind [cittassa ekaggataā]' in many discourses. The commentaries explained this one-pointedness as an object (PsA.230) and the object of mind nearing concentration as a counterpart sign [paṭibhāga-nimitta].

Samatha is a state in which the mind is focused on an object called a sign. According to all the commentary literature including the Path of Purification, such concentration is developed through access-concentration [upacāra-samādhi] and absorption-concentration [appanā-samādhi]. (Vis.IV.31–33) The *Comprehensive Manual of the Abhidhamma* explains the concentration practice in further detail as preparatory, access, and absorption concentration.

First, the preparatory practice is the elementary practice done prior to the arising of access-concentration. Specifically, the preparatory practice is the state up to or immediately prior to the arising of a counterpart sign while the five hindrances are suppressed. Access-concentration occurs when the five hindrances are suppressed and from the time a counterpart sign appears, immediately prior to the arising of the mind of gotrabhū,[5] while entering the state of jhāna. The absorption-concentration is the mind that arises right after the mind of gotrabhū; it means the states of the first jhāna through the fourth jhāna.

Unlike this, vipassanā is a practice that enables one to see clearly the momentary arising and passing away of dhamma and is not a practice in which one focuses on a sign; therefore,

---

5 The gotrabhū is one who has entered the lineage of the Noble Ones.

a counterpart sign does not arise. Since a counterpart sign does not arise, there is no absorption-concentration in the vipassanā practice. Of course, without a high level of concentration, it is impossible to see an object thoroughly as impermanent, suffering, and non-self. Therefore, the high level of concentration during the vipassanā practice cannot be called absorption-concentration. The commentary literature such as the Path of Purification calls the high level of concentration that occurs during the vipassanā practice momentary-concentration [khaṇika-samādhi].

The Path of Purification calls the practitioner who does not practice samatha first but practices vipassanā right away, a 'dry vipassanā practitioner' or a 'pure vipassanā practitioner.' Momentary-concentration is a highly-focused state that occurs during this pure vipassanā practice; it is said to be equal to access-concentration or comparable to the first jhāna of the samatha practice. Thus, there is a basis for concentration in the vipassanā practice.

"Concentration is the mind being focused on one-pointedness. The concentration achieved through samatha is called access-concentration or absorption-concentration; the high-level concentration of vipassanā is called momentary-concentration."

❧ CHAPTER 8

The Threefold Training in Morality, Concentration, and Wisdom

The Threefold Training: Three Kinds of Training

All the Buddhist practices of the past 2,600 years can be summed up as the threefold training in morality, concentration, and wisdom. The Buddha emphasized the threefold training in many places within the Early Buddhist discourses. The threefold training [tissosikkhā] can be translated as practicing three kinds of training: morality [sīla], concentration [samādhi], and wisdom [paññā]. In Chinese, this is also translated as morality-concentration-wisdom, the threefold training; consequently, they are very well known to Koreans. Morality means living a moral life, concentration means practicing concentration meditation, and wisdom means developing insight.

The threefold training – morality, concentration, and wisdom – is emphasized in many places in the Early Buddhist discourses as a must-practice for a Buddhist. In the *Chanting Together Discourse*

(D33), it is said there are, "three kinds of training in higher morality, higher mind, and higher wisdom." (D33)

Also, in the *Samaṇa Discourse*, it is stated, "Bhikkhus, there are these three samaṇa tasks to be practiced by an samaṇa. What three? 1) The undertaking of the training in the higher morality, 2) the undertaking of training in the higher mind, and 3) the undertaking of training in the higher wisdom. These are the three samaṇa tasks to be practiced by an samaṇa." (A3:81)

In the commentary of the Dīgha Nikāya, it is explained that of the threefold training, morality training is mainly covered in the Vinaya Piṭaka [the Collection of Rules of Conduct], concentration training is covered in the Sutta Piṭaka [the Collection of Discourses], and wisdom training is covered in the Abhidhamma Piṭaka [the Collection of Higher Teaching]. (DA.i.19) It is further stated that, "Morality means following the five and ten precepts and the restraint of the rules is called the higher morality. The eight stages of attainment refer to mind [concentration] and Jhāna, the basis of vipassanā is called the higher mind. Wisdom in regard to the fact that kamma is one's master is insight and insight of vipassanā is called the higher insight." (DA.iii.1003)

The commentary of the Majjhima Nikāya said, "Morality is the fourfold purity of morality. Concentration is the eight stages of attainment which is the basis of vipassanā. Insight can be mundane or supramundane." (Ma.ii.147)

Also, traditionally the noble eightfold path is explained in the context of the threefold training. The Saṁyutta Nikāya explains as follows:

"Here, the path [magga] means the noble eightfold path and is practiced for realization. Morality [sīla] includes right speech, right action, and right livelihood. Concentration [samādhi] includes right effort, right mindfulness, and right concentration. Wisdom [paññā] includes right view and right intention." (SA.i.170)

"Morality training means living a moral life, concentration training means practicing concentration meditation, and wisdom training means developing insight."

The Threefold Training: Morality, Concentration, and Wisdom Training

Let's examine the content of morality, concentration, and wisdom training in detail.

First, what is the training in morality?

There are four kinds of morality: morality in regard to the restraint of the rules, the restraint of the senses, the purity in one's means of livelihood, and the requisites.

1. morality in regard to the restraint of rules means perfectly observing the five, eight, bhikkhu, and bhikkhuni precepts. The five and eight precepts apply to lay Buddhists. There are 227 precepts for bhikkhus and 311 precepts for bhikkhunis.
2. morality in regard to the restraint of the senses means maintaining mindfulness while coming in contact with the objects of the senses, preventing the mind from running to pleasurable objects or stirring with hatred toward the unpleasurable objects.
3. morality in regard to the purity in one's means of livelihood refers to maintaining livelihood through right means.
4. morality in regard to the requisites means always using the four necessities [clothing, food, lodging, and medicine] reflecting on the purpose of their use in homeless life.

The core of morality training is restraint [saṁvara]. In various places of the Early Buddhist discourses, accomplishment of rules is defined as follows:

"And how is a bhikkhu accomplished in virtuous behavior? Here, a bhikkhu is virtuous; he dwells restrained by the Pāṭimokkha,[1] possessed of good conduct and resort, seeing

---

1 The Pāṭimokkha is the monastic rules of conduct for bhikkhus and bhik-

danger in minute faults. Having undertaken the training rules, he trains in them." (A4:37, The Non-Decline Discourse)

In chapter one of the Path of Purification, morality is presented with emphasis on restraint. The core of the training is restraint. Let's compare this to a refrigerator. If the door is not closed securely, all the sumptuous food stored in the refrigerator would be spoiled. Likewise, if one does not restrain one's six sensory doors, even if one possesses various supernormal power born of the first jhāna to the attainment of neither perception nor non-perception and also attains the wisdom through insight of the impermanence·suffering·non-self, all would be useless. Therefore, restraint is the core of morality training.

Second, what is the training in concentration?

It is the focusing of the mind on one object. In Chinese, this is translated as 心一境性 [one-pointedness of mind]. In many discourses, concentration or the training in concentration is defined as one-pointedness of mind. Here, the 'point' means the object (PsA.230). The right concentration in the Early Buddhist discourses always refers to the four jhānas, from the first to fourth.

The stock phrases for the four jhānas that appear in various places in the Early Buddhist discourses are as follows:

"Here, bhikkhus, secluded from sensual pleasures, secluded from unwholesome states, a bhikkhu enters and dwells in the first jhāna, which is accompanied by applied thought and sustained thought, with rapture and happiness born of seclusion. With the subsiding of applied thought and sustained thought, he enters and dwells in the second jhāna, which has internal confidence and unification of mind, is without applied thought and sustained thought, and has rapture and happiness born of concentration. With the fading away as well of rapture, he dwells equanimous and, mindful and clearly

khunis of the Buddhist order.

155

comprehending, he experiences happiness with the body; he enters and dwells in the third jhāna of which the noble ones declare: 'He is equanimous, mindful, one who dwells happily.' With the abandoning of pleasure and pain, and with the previous passing away of joy and displeasure, he enters and dwells in the fourth jhāna, which is neither-painful-nor-pleasant and includes the purification of mindfulness by equanimity." (S45:8, The Analysis Discourse)

As seen here, the key words that are used to describe the first jhāna through the fourth jhāna have these five components of concentration: applied thought [vitakka], sustained thought [vicāra], rapture [pīti], happiness [sukha], and one-pointedness of mind [cittassa ekaggata] plus the sixth, equanimity [upekkahā].

"In this way, among the four jhānas, the first jhāna has the characteristic of the five mental formations: applied thought, sustained thought, rapture, happiness, and concentration; with elimination of applied thought and sustained thought, the second jhāna has rapture, happiness, and concentration; with the fading away of rapture, the third jhāna has happiness and concentration; in the fourth jhāna, happiness is abandoned and equanimity is established instead, and therefore only equanimity and concentration remain." (Vis.III.21)

Third, what is the training in wisdom?

It is insight [wisdom]. The Pāli word, paññā has been translated in Chinese as wisdom [慧] and was transliterated as banya [반야] in Korean. In the Path of Purification, it is explained, "Insight [paññā] has the characteristic of penetrating [paṭivedha] the individual essences of states." (Vis.XIV.7) In the Early Buddhist discourses, ignorance is defined as not penetrating the Four Noble Truths; the higher knowledge [vijjā] is defined as penetrating the Four Noble Truths. This is also the content of insight.

In the Early Buddhist discourses, the wisdom training appears as six supernormal powers, the threefold higher knowledge, the eight supernormal powers, the knowledge of the destruction of the taints, etc. The six supernormal powers are as follows:

1. Knowledge of supernormal psychic powers [iddhividha-ñāṇa]
2. Knowledge of divine ear [dibbasota-ñāṇa]
3. Knowledge of penetration of the mind of others [cetopariya-ñāṇa]
4. Knowledge of recollection of former life [pubbenivāsa-anussati-ñāṇa]
5. Knowledge of divine eye [dibbacakkhu-ñāṇa]
6. Knowledge of destruction of the taints [āsavakkhaya-ñāṇa]

Among these, the above 4), 5), and 6) are called the threefold higher knowledge [te-vijjā]. When the two factors 'knowing and seeing [wisdom of vipassana]' and 'mind-made body' are added to the six supernormal powers, they become the eight supernormal powers. (D2, etc.) There are also discourses that only show 6) above.

Among the six supernormal powers, the threefold higher knowledge, and the eight supernormal powers, the core of the wisdom training is the knowledge of destruction of the taints; the core of the knowledge of destruction of the taints means thoroughly penetrating the Four Noble Truths; this is the content of the right view of the noble eightfold path. The ignorance of the 12 links of dependent origination is not knowing the Four Noble Truths; knowing the Four Noble Truths is the training in wisdom – in other words, the core of insight. Therefore, the right view [of Buddhism], the higher knowledge [vijjā], and the insight can all be summarized as knowing the Four Noble Truths. This is the core of the training in wisdom.

"The core of the training in morality: restraint.
The training in concentration: one-pointedness of mind.
The training in wisdom: insight of the Four Noble Truths."

The Threefold Training: The Stock Phrases for Morality, Concentration, and Wisdom

In many places within the Early Buddhist discourses, the Buddha's most important instruction is defined as the threefold training: morality, concentration, and wisdom – the three aggregates.

In 12 of the 13 discourses included in the first volume of the Dīgha Nikāya, the Buddha spoke of the main frame of Buddhism as the threefold training: morality, concentration, and wisdom. These teachings are detailed in 23 stock phrases. In the *Subha Discourse* (D10), instead of the word, 'training [sikkhā]' of morality, concentration, and wisdom, the word, 'aggregate [kkhandha]' of morality, concentration, and wisdom is used; however, the meaning is the same. Likewise, in many places within the Early Buddhist discourses, the Buddha's teaching means the threefold training in morality, concentration, and wisdom – the three aggregates.

Now, let's examine the 24-step stock phrases of morality, concentration, and wisdom from volume one of the Dīgha Nikāya.

1. "A Tathāgata arises in the world ... He teaches the Dhamma which is lovely in its beginning, lovely in its middle, lovely in its ending, in the spirit and in the letter, and displays the fully-perfected and purified holy life ...

2. This Dhamma is heard by a householder or a householder's son, or one reborn in some family or other. . . . shaves off his hair and beard, dons yellow robes and goes forth into the homeless life ...

3. And having gone forth, he dwells restrained by the restraint of the rules ...

4. The Short Section on Morality Discourse – 26 Precepts ...

5. The Middle Section on Morality – Refrain from the Ten Wrongful Actions ...

6. The Large Section on Morality – Refrain from the Seven Wrong Livelihood...

7. That monk who is perfected in morality sees no danger from any side...

8. A monk is a guardian of the sense-doors...

9. A monk is accomplished in mindfulness and clear awareness...

10. A monk is contented with [requisites]...

11. Finds a solitary lodging...

12. Abandoning worldly desires ... abandoning ill-will and hatred... abandoning sloth-and-torpor... abandoning worry-and-flurry ... abandoning doubt, he dwells with doubt left behind... [Abandoning five hindrances]

13. Enters and remains in the first jhāna...

14. Enters and remains in the second jhāna...

15. Enters and remains in the third jhāna...

16. Enters and remains in the fourth jhāna...

17. Directs and inclines his mind towards knowing and seeing...

18. Directs and inclines his mind to the production of a mind-made body...

19. Applies and directs his mind to the various supernormal psychic powers...

20. Applies and directs his mind to the divine ear...

21. Applies and directs his mind to the knowledge of penetration of others' minds...

22. Applies and directs his mind to the knowledge of recollection of former life...

23. Applies and directs his mind to the knowledge of the divine eye...

24. Applies and directs his mind to the knowledge of destruction of the taints ... He knows as it really is ... 'Birth is finished, the holy life has been led, done is what had to be done, there is nothing further here.'" (D1.2, the Sāmaññaphala Discourse)

Among these, the venerable Ananda classified 1) through 7) as the aggregates of morality, 8) through 16) as the aggregates of concentration, and 17) through 24) as the aggregates of insight.

Here, the core of the concentration aggregates is mindfulness, clear awareness, abandoning the five hindrances, and attaining first to fourth jhānas; the core of the insight aggregates is the threefold higher knowledge.

"In the Early Buddhist discourses, the teaching of the Buddha is the threefold training in morality, concentration, and wisdom – the three aggregates."

The Threefold Training: Piles of Five Kinds of Dhamma

The threefold training or the three kinds of learning is the training in morality, concentration, and wisdom. Adding deliverance [vimutti] and the knowledge and vision of liberation [vimuttiñāṇa-dassana] to the threefold training, they become the five aggregates of Dhamma [pañca dhamma-kkhandhā]. In the various Early Buddhist discourses the five aggregates of Dhamma appear as the aggregates of morality, concentration, wisdom, deliverance, and the knowledge and vision of liberation. (S3:24) This became the technical term, "the five aggregates [branches] of Dhamma" in the *Expanding Decades Discourse*. (D34)

The five aggregates of morality, concentration, wisdom, deliverance, and knowledge and vision of liberation are very familiar teachings to Koreans. Because the Koreans' morning and evening Buddhist chanting services include the five kinds of incense or fragrance, corresponding with the five-part Dharma body (Dharmakaya)[2] – the fragrance of morality, concentration, wisdom, deliverance, and knowledge and vision of liberation.

Then among these, what is deliverance? Experiencing Nibbāna is deliverance. In the Early Buddhist discourses, deliverance means attainment of the Arahantship, realization of Nibbāna, or broadly, attainment of the four kinds of fruition: the fruition of stream-entry, once-returning, non-returning, and Arahantship. Without experiencing these stages of the noble ones, there is no deliverance.

The four kinds of fruition – the fruition of stream-entry, once-returning, non-returning, and Arahantship – can only be realized when one experiences Nibbāna, even for a moment.

---

2 The Dharmakāya is one of the three bodies [trikaya] of the Buddha in Mahāyāna Buddhism.

Therefore, deliverance is only possible when one has experienced Nibbāna, even for a moment.

What is the knowledge and vision of liberation? It is retrospective knowledge. There is no specific information about what the knowledge and vision of liberation means in the discourses. Therefore, for the meaning of the knowledge and vision of liberation, one must look in the commentaries. Stated in various commentaries, the knowledge and vision of liberation means retrospective knowledge [paccavekkhaṇa-ñāṇa]. Several commentaries state that "'the knowledge and vision of liberation' includes the 19 kinds of retrospective knowledge [paccavekkhaṇa-ñāṇa]." (MA.ii.147, etc.)

According to the Path of Purification, there are five kinds of reviews: 1) the review of the path, 2) the review of the fruition, 3) the review of the defilements, 4) the review of the remaining defilements, 5) the review of Nibbāna. Because the Arahant does not have the review of the remaining defilements, there are 19 kinds[3] of review for the noble ones from the stream-enterer to the Arahant.

The following is a quote from the Path of Purification:

1. "He reviews the path in this way, 'So this is the path I have come by.'
2. Next, he reviews the fruition after that in this way, 'This is the blessing I have obtained.'
3. Next, he reviews the defilements that have been abandoned, 'These are the defilements abandoned in me.'
4. Next, he reviews the defilements still to be eliminated by the three higher paths, 'These are the defilements still remaining in me.'
5. Lastly he reviews the deathless Nibbāna in this way, 'This is the state [dhamma] that has been penetrated by me as object.'

---

3 (4 kinds of noble one x 5 kinds of review) – (1 Arahant) = 19 kinds of review

So the noble disciple who is a stream-enterer has five kinds of reviewing. . . . the Arahant has no reviewing of remaining defilement. So all the kinds of reviewing total nineteen." (Vis. XXII.20–21)

Because the Buddha's teaching or Dhamma is summarized as the five kinds – morality, concentration, wisdom, deliverance, and knowledge and vision of liberation – they are called the aggregates of Dhamma in the Early Buddhist discourses.

"By adding deliverance and knowledge and vision of liberation to the threefold training – the training in morality, concentration, and wisdom – they become the five aggregates of Dhamma."

The Threefold Training: The Seven Stages of Purification

If the threefold training in morality, concentration, and wisdom are the key words of the Buddhist training emphasized in the Early Buddhist discourses, the seven stages of purification [visuddhi] is an important teaching of Theravada Buddhism that explains the training structure and the theory. The subjects of the seven stages of purification are: 1) purification of morality, 2) purification of mind, 3) purification of view, 4) purification by overcoming doubt, 5) purification by knowledge and vision of what is path and not path, 6) purification by knowledge and vision of the way, and 7) purification by knowledge and vision.

As seen here, the seven stages of purification correspond to the threefold training in morality, concentration, and wisdom. Wisdom is further emphasized by splitting it into the five stages of purification to make up the seven stages of purification in total. The Path of Purification, a comprehensive commentary of the four Nikāyas, explains the Buddha's authentic teachings by adopting these two methods. In the Path of Purification, chapters one and two contain the training in morality and the purification of morality; chapters three through 13 apply to the training in concentration and the purification of mind; chapters 14 through 23 explain the training in wisdom. Among these, chapters 18 through 22 contain the explanations about the five stages of purification from the purification of view to the purification by knowledge and vision.

The seven stages of purification appear in the Nikāyas. In the *Relay Chariots Discourse* (M24) of the Majjhima Nikāya, the seven stages of purification are compared to the seven relay chariots. It is explained that just as one arrives at the destination by means of the relay chariots, the practitioner arrives at Nibbāna by relying on the seven stages of purification, one after another.

1. The purification of morality [sīla-visuddhi] is an excellent possession of the fourfold purity of morality: restraint with regard to the rules, sense-restraint, purity of livelihood, and morality with regard to the four requisites.

2. The purification of mind [citta-visuddhi] means obtaining the access-concentration and the absorption-concentration by overcoming the five hindrances: sensual desire, ill-will, sloth and torpor, restlessness and remorse, and doubt.

3. The purification of view [diṭṭhi-visuddhi] is the insight of the characteristics of mentality and materiality or the five aggregates that make up beings. The purification of view is purifying the wrong view by clearly understanding 'the self' and 'the world' through the teachings of the five aggregates, the 12 sense bases, and the 18 elements.

4. The purification by overcoming doubt [kankhā-vitaraṇa-visuddhi] is the establishment of wisdom developed by knowing the cause and condition of mentality and materiality and overcoming doubt regarding the three periods of time: past, present, and future. It is understanding that the mentality and materiality that make up 'I' and 'the world' do not arise by chance or by some hypothetical cause and certainly are not created by a god, but that all things are interdependent and dependently arisen.

    The Path of Purification praises highly the one who eliminates doubt by clearly knowing the cause and condition of the five aggregates or mentality and materiality as a 'lesser stream-enterer.' (Vis.XIX.27) If the previous purification of view is clearly knowing the Dhamma of the Abhidhamma, the purification by overcoming doubt is clearly knowing all Dhammas' interrelationships and interdependence, and clearly comprehending the teaching of dependent origination – which explains the origin and cessation of suffering.

5. The purification by knowledge and vision of what is path and not-path [maggāmagga-ñāṇa-dassana-visuddhi] means defin-

ing the characteristic of the path and not-path by knowing
the ten imperfections of insight: illumination, rapture, calmness, faith, energy, bliss, knowledge, assurance, equanimity,
and attachment. This purification is knowledge established
through knowing that illumination and so forth are not-path.
Insight of the impermanence·suffering·non-self is the path.

6. The purification by knowledge and vision of the way [paṭipadā-
ñāṇa-dassana-visuddhi] refers to nine kinds of knowledge
from the knowledge of arising and passing away to the knowledge in conformity.

    In general, there are ten kinds of knowledge arising from
practicing vipassanā: 1) knowledge of meditation, 2) knowledge of arising and passing away, 3) knowledge of dissolution,
4) knowledge of terror, 5) knowledge of danger, 6) knowledge
of disgust, 7) knowledge of desire for deliverance, 8) knowledge of re-observation, 9) knowledge of equanimity about
formations, and 10) knowledge in conformity.

    Among these, the first stage, the knowledge of meditation
and the knowledge of arising and passing away [weak stage]
are known to belong to the purification by knowledge and
vision of what is path and not-path. The remaining nine
stages – from the knowledge of arising and passing away
[mature stage] to the tenth stage, the knowledge in conformity – belong to the purification by knowledge and vision of
the way.

7. Purification by knowledge and vision [ñāṇa-dassana-visuddhi]
refers to the four supramundane paths – the path to stream-entry, once-returning, non-returning, and Arahantship – and
the wisdom of the four supramundane paths. At this stage,
vipassanā is completed as the path and the fruit.

    The Path of Purification and other commentaries explain
these seven stages of purification as very important steps
in realizing liberation. This agrees with the method of the
threefold training in morality, concentration, and wisdom.

The purification of morality corresponds to the training in morality. The purification of mind corresponds to the training in concentration. The purification of view, the purification by overcoming doubt, the purification by knowledge and vision of what is path and not-path, the purification by knowledge and vision of the way, and the purification by knowledge and vision correspond to the training in wisdom. In the seven stages of purification, the training in wisdom is explained in detail by further categorizing it into five stages. This is an expanded version of the vipassanā practice which is emphasized in the Early Buddhist discourses.

"As one would arrive at a destination by means of relay chariots, the practitioner would arrive at Nibbāna by relying on the seven stages of purification, one after another."

⚜ CHAPTER 9
The Noble Ones Who Extinguished All Fetters

The Ten Fetters and Four Kinds of Noble Ones

In the Early Buddhist discourses, humans are broadly separated into two categories, ordinary people [puthujjana] and noble ones [ariya]. The ordinary person is unenlightened and the noble one is enlightened. The noble ones are further divided into four categories: the stream-enterer, once-returner, non-returner, and Arahant. Because the stream-enterer, once-returner, and non-returner need further training, they are called learners [sekha]; because the Arahants have extinguished all fetters and no further training is needed, they are called those who have finished training [asekha].

What is the basis for classifying the noble ones into four categories: the stream-enterer, once-returner, non-returner, and Arahant? The Buddha spoke of the ten fetters [saṁyojana] in various places in the Early Buddhist discourses. Depending on how many of the ten fetters have been abandoned, the noble ones are divided into four categories such as the stream-enterer, once-returner, etc. (A7:15, etc.)

The ten fetters are as follows:

1. Self-view [sakkāya-diṭṭhi]: Attachment to a fundamentally wrong view that a permanent and unchanging self or an entity exists – holding the 20 wrong views[1] about the five aggregates that the self exists: thinking the five aggregates are the self, the self possesses the five aggregates, the five aggregates are in the self, the self is in the five aggregates, etc.
2. Attachment to moral precepts and religious ritual [sīlabbata-parāmāsa]: Attachment to rules and rituals thinking one can be liberated by merely keeping them.
3. Doubt [vicikicchā]: Doubting the Buddha, Dhamma, Sangha, precepts, dependent origination, etc.
4. Sensual lust [kāma-rāga]: The five cords of sensual lust for sensual pleasure of eye, ear, nose, tongue, and body.
5. Ill will [byāpāda]: Hatred, resentment, hostility, and angry mind.
6. Attachment to the form spheres [rūpa-rāga]: Delighting in the higher states from the first jhāna to the fourth jhāna.
7. Attachment to the formless spheres [arūpa-rāga]: Delighting in the higher states from the base of boundless space to the base of neither perception nor non-perception.
8. Conceit or self-measurement [māna]: Thoughts such as 'I am superior to others, I am equal to others, and I am inferior to others.'
9. Restlessness [uddhacca]: Restless and anxious mind.
10. Ignorance [avijjā]: Not knowing the Four Noble Truths.

Among the above ten fetters, the first five [self-view, attachment to moral precepts and religious ritual, doubt, sensual lust, and ill will] are called the lower fetters since these bind the aggregates that are originated in the sensual-desire sphere. The

---

1 The 20 wrong views refer to four modes of wrong view about the five aggregates. $4 \times 5 = 20$

remaining five [attachment to the form spheres, attachment to the formless spheres, conceit or self-measurement, restlessness, and ignorance] are called the higher fetters since these bind the aggregates that are originated in the form and formless spheres.

In various places of the Abhidhamma literature, it is stated that the first three among the ten fetters are to be abandoned by seeing. The other seven are to be abandoned by development. (Dhs.183) Seeing and development are technical terms used in such places as in the path of seeing [dassana-magga], the path of development [bhāvanā-magga], and in many other places in the commentary literature. (MS.i.75) It is explained that one becomes the stream-enterer by the path of seeing. Depending on the level of accomplishment of the path of development, one becomes the once-returner, non-returner, and Arahant in order. (Ps.ii.82)

The path of seeing and the path of development are treated as important subjects throughout generations of Buddhism. They are discussed in the representative literature, such as the *Abhidharma Storehouse Treatise* [Abhidharmakośa-bhāṣya] of the Northern Abhidharma and the *Discourse on the Theory of Consciousness-only* [Vijñaptimātratāsiddhi-śāstra] of the Yogācāra literature.

In the Early Buddhist discourses, the stream-enterer is a noble one who has abandoned the three fetters of self-view, attachment to rules and ritual, and doubt; the once-returner is a noble one who has not only abandoned the previous three fetters but also weakened the two fetters of sensual lust and ill will. The non-returner is a noble one who has completely abandoned the lower five fetters; the Arahant is a noble one who has abandoned all ten fetters. (A7:15, etc.)

"Depending on how many fetters one has abandoned, a noble one is classified into one of four categories: the stream-enterer, once-returner, non-returner, or Arahant."

Buddhism and the Cycle of Rebirth

Buddhism is a teaching that is based on the non-self. In many places in the Early Buddhist discourses, the non-self of all conditioned phenomena is emphasized. The self-view is the wrong view of thinking a self exists with respect to the five aggregates. If one does not abandon this wrong view, one cannot become a stream-enterer, which is the first stage of liberation, even if one has experienced the superior states of concentration and can use supernormal powers at will.

Although the non-self is the basic teaching of Buddhism, transmigration or the cycle of rebirth is also emphasized in many places in Early Buddhism. The cycle of rebirth is a translation of saṁsāra. The literal meaning of saṁsāra is 'moving together or flowing together.' In Chinese, this has been typically translated as transmigration, wheel-turning, transmigration through birth and death, and birth and death. According to these literal meanings, saṁsāra is closer to 'a flow' based on dependent origination rather than the Hinduism's reincarnation theory of re-embodiment of the self.

The non-self and transmigration, at a glance, seem to be mutually contradictory teachings. As a result, those with misunderstanding about Buddhism insist that the Buddha did not teach the cycle of rebirth due to the contradictory aspect of transmigration of non-self. However, the Buddha did teach the cycle of rebirth in many places in the Early Buddhist discourses. He taught about transmigration and a way to escape from it.

Above all, one must understand the difference between transmigration of Buddhism and reincarnation of Hinduism. In the Hinduism's reincarnation theory, the non-changing self [ātman] exists and this self goes through re-embodiment from this life to the next. Re-embodiment means that the self exists in the heart and upon death of this body, the self inhabits another body in the next life. This can be called 'reincarnation of the self.'

Unlike the above, in Buddhism, continuity [santati] of this life is connected to that of the next life, and rebirth occurs; this rebirth is called transmigration. In the commentaries, the continuous and endless unfolding of the five aggregates, the 12 sense bases, and the 18 elements is called transmigration. Therefore, the transmigration of Buddhism means the flow of dependent origination of all conditioned phenomena that arise, pass away, and change based on conditions. The transmigration of Buddhism is the transmigration of the flow of dependent origination without the subject or the main constituent and also can be called 'the transmigration of the non-self.'

Transmigration is the flow of the momentary arising and passing away. Basically, the arising and passing away of the five aggregates that unfold each moment is transmigration. (DA.ii.496; SA.ii.97) Viewed from the stance of birth and death, the death consciousness [cūti-citta] arises and passes away, then conditioned by this, the rebirth-linking consciousness [paṭisandhi-viññāṇa] arises. This is the transmigration. The constant arising and passing away of the five aggregates in each and every moment, flowing to the next life, is the transmigration.

The cause for the transmigration is craving and ignorance. That is why the Buddha stated, 'Craving is what leads to rebirth [ponobhāvikā].' He said ignorance is the fundamental cause for rebirth in the 12 links of dependent origination. As long as craving and ignorance exist, the flow of transmigration continues. Of course, there is no re-becoming, rebirth, or transmigration for the Arahant. Therefore, except for the Arahant, all beings' transmigrations are described as natural events in many places of the Early Buddhist discourses.

Transmigration is certainly not a metaphor. It is the most vivid picture of sentient beings, running around and floating along, wrapped up in craving and ignorance. Therefore, one should not be swayed by the incorrect assumption that Buddhism does not acknowledge transmigration. The Buddha's song of victory in the

Old Age of the Dhammapada also reveals clearly transmigration and the cessation of transmigration:

"Through many a birth in saṁsāra have I wandered in vain, seeking the builder of this house. Repeated birth is indeed suffering!

"O house-builder, you are seen! You will not build this house again. For your rafters are broken and your ridgepole shattered. My mind has reached the unconditioned; I have attained the destruction of craving." (Dhp.153–154)

"The transmigration of Buddhism means the flow of dependent origination of all conditioned phenomena that arise, pass away, and change based on conditions. This is the flow of dependent origination and is called 'the transmigration of the non-self.'**"**

Appendix 1: Five Aggregates

Five Aggregates: Pañca-khandha			
Material form, matter, materiality: Rūpa	Name, mentality: Nāma		
	Mental factors, mental, mental concomitants: Cetasikā		Mind, cognizance, consciousness: Citta
	Feeling: Vedanā	Perception: Saññā	Mental Formations: Saṅkhārā	Consciousness: Viññāṇa

Appendix 2: The Four Groups and 82 Dhammas of Theravada Buddhism

<table>
<tr><td colspan="4" align="center">All Phenomena: Sabbe dhammā</td></tr>
<tr>
<td colspan="3" align="center">Conditioned Phenomena: Saṅkhara-dhammā</td>
<td>Unconditioned Phenomenon:</td>
</tr>
<tr>
<td>I. Mind, cognizance, consciousness: Citta</td>
<td>II. Mental factors, mental, mental concomitants: Cetasikā</td>
<td>III. Material form, matter, materiality: Rūpa</td>
<td>IV. Extinction of lust, hatred, and delusion: Nibbāna</td>
</tr>
<tr>
<td>ONE TYPE</td>
<td>52 TYPES
1. Mental factors that become common with others [13 types]
2. Unwholesome mental factors [14 types]
3. Beautiful mental factors [25 types]</td>
<td>28 TYPES
1. Produced materiality: Nipphanna-rūpa [18 types]
2. Unproduced materiality: Anipphanna-rūpa [10 types]

*Excluding the ten unproduced materiality, the 72 types are the ultimate realities: paramattha-dhamma</td>
<td>ONE TYPE</td>
</tr>
<tr>
<td>CONSCIOUS-NESS: Viññāṇa</td>
<td>FEELING: Vedanā
PERCEPTION: Saññā
MENTAL FORMATIONS: Saṅkhārā</td>
<td>MATERIAL FORM, MATTER, MATERIALITY: Rūpa</td>
<td></td>
</tr>
</table>

Appendix 3: 28 Types of Materiality

Produced materiality: Nipphanna-rūpa [18 types]		Basic elements: Bhūta-rūpa	1	Earth element: Paṭhavī-dhātu	Basic elements: Bhūta-rūpa [4 types]
			2	Water element: Āpo-dhātu	
			3	Fire element: Tejo-dhātu	
			4	Wind element: Vāyo-dhātu	
		Sensitivity materiality: Pasāda-rūpa	5	Eye sensitivity: Cakkhu-pasāda	Derived materiality: Upādāya-rūpa [24 types]
			6	Ear sensitivity: Sota-pasāda	
			7	Nose sensitivity: Ghāna-pasāda	
			8	Tongue sensitivity: Jivhā-pasāda	
			9	Body sensitivity: Kāya-pasāda	
		Objective materiality: Gacara-rūpa	10	Visible form: Rūpa	
			11	Sound: Sadda	
			12	Odor: Gandha	
			13	Taste or flavor: Rasa	
				*Since tangible is not an element of its own, but is an element of earth, fire, and wind of the four great elements, it is excluded from the objective materiality.	
		Sex materiality: Bhāva-rūpa	14	Female sex-materiality: Itthibhāva or itthaīa	
			15	Male sex-materiality: Pumbhāva or purisatta	
		Heart materiality: Hadaya-rūpa	16	Heart-basis: Hadaya-vatthu	
		Life materiality: Jīvita-rūpa	17	Life faculty: Jīvitindriya	
		Nutriment materiality: Āhāra-rūpa	18	Nutritive essence: Ojā	
Unproduced materiality: Anipphanna-rūpa [Ten types]		Delimitation materiality: Pariccheda-rūpa	19	Space element: Ākāsa-dhātu	
		Intimation materiality: Viññatti-rūpa	20	Bodily intimation: Kāya-viññatti	
			21	Verbal intimation: Vacī-viññatti	
		Alteration materiality: Vikāra-rūpa	22	Lightness of materiality: Rūpassa lahutā	
			23	Malleability of materiality: Rūpassa mudutā	
			24	Wieldiness of materiality: Rūpassa kammaññatā	
		Characteristic materiality: Lakkhaṇa-rūpa	25	Growth of materiality: Upacaya	
			26	Continuity of materiality: Santati	
			27	Aging of materiality: Jaratā	
			28	Impermanence of materiality: Aniccatā	

Appendix 4: The 89/121 Types of Consciousness of Theravada Buddhism [1/2] Y=Yes, N=No

		Unwholesome consciousness [12]	Wholesome consciousness [21]	Resultant consciousness [36]	Root-cause	Rebirth-linking [19]	Registration [11]	Functional consciousness [20]
Mundane consciousness	Sensual-desire sphere [54]	Rooted in lust [8]		Unwholesome resultant [7]				
		1. Joy, views-Y, prompted-N		13. Equanimity, eye consciousness				
		2. Joy, views-Y, prompted-Y		14. Equanimity, ear consciousness				
		3. Joy, views-N, prompted-N		15. Equanimity, nose consciousness				
		4. Joy, views-N, prompted-Y		16. Equanimity, tongue consciousness				
		5. Equanimity, views-Y, prompted-N		17. Painful, body consciousness				
		6. Equanimity, views-Y, prompted-Y		18. Equanimity, receiving consciousness				
		7. Equanimity, views-N, prompted-N		19. Equanimity, investigating consciousness [rebirth-linking, registration]		Y	Y	
		8. Equanimity, views-N, prompted-Y		Wholesome resultant [8]				
				20. Equanimity, eye consciousness				Rootless functional [3]
		Rooted in hatred [2]		21. Equanimity, ear consciousness				28. Equanimity, Five-sense-door adverting consciousness
		9. Grief, resentment, prompted-N		22. Equanimity, nose consciousness				29. Equanimity, Mind-door adverting consciousness
		10. Grief, resentment, prompted-Y		23. Equanimity, tongue consciousness				30. Joy, Smile-producing consciousness
				24. Pleasant, body consciousness				
		Rooted in delusion [2]		25. Equanimity, receiving consciousness				
		11. Equanimity, uncertainty		26. Joy, investigating consciousness			Y	
		12. Equanimity, agitation		27. Equanimity, investigating consciousness		Y	Y	

Appendix 4: The 89/121 Types of Consciousness of Theravada Buddhism [2/2] Y=Yes, N=No

| | | Unwholesome consciousness [12] | Wholesome consciousness [21] | Indeterminate consciousness [56] | | | | |
| | | | | Resultant consciousness [36] | | | | Functional consciousness (20) |
					Root-cause	Rebirth-linking [19]	Registration [11]	
Mundane consciousness	Sensual-desire sphere [54]		Sensual-desire sphere, wholesome [8]	Sensual-desire sphere, resultant [8]				Sensual-desire sphere, functional [8]
			31. Joy, knowledge-Y, prompted-N	39. Joy, knowledge-Y, prompted-N	3	Y	Y	47. Joy, knowledge-Y, prompted-N
			32. Joy, knowledge-Y, prompted-Y	40. Joy, knowledge-Y, prompted-Y	3	Y	Y	48. Joy, knowledge-Y, prompted-Y
			33. Joy, knowledge-N, prompted-Y	41. Joy, knowledge-N, prompted-Y	2	Y	Y	49. Joy, knowledge-N, prompted-N
			34. Joy, knowledge-N, prompted-Y	42. Joy, knowledge-N, prompted-Y	2	Y	Y	50. Joy, knowledge-N, prompted-Y
			35. Joy, knowledge-Y, prompted-N	43. Joy, knowledge-Y, prompted-N	3	Y	Y	51. Joy, knowledge-Y, prompted-N
			36. Joy, knowledge-Y, prompted-Y	44. Joy, knowledge-Y, prompted-Y	3	Y	Y	52. Joy, knowledge-Y, prompted-Y
			37. Joy, knowledge-N, prompted-N	45. Joy, knowledge-N, prompted-N	2	Y	Y	53. Joy, knowledge-N, prompted-N
			38. Joy, knowledge-N, prompted-Y	46. Joy, knowledge-N, prompted-Y	2	Y	Y	54. Joy, knowledge-N, prompted-Y
	Form sphere [15]		55. First Jhāna	60. First Jhāna	3	Y		65. First Jhāna
			56. Second Jhāna	61. Second Jhāna	3	Y		66. Second Jhāna
			57. Third Jhāna	62. Third Jhāna	3	Y		67. Third Jhāna
			58. Fourth Jhāna	63. Fourth Jhāna	3	Y		68. Fourth Jhāna
			59. Fifth Jhāna	64. Fifth Jhāna	3	Y		69. Fifth Jhāna
	Formless sphere [12]		70. The base of boundless space	74. The base of boundless space	3	Y		78. The base of boundless space
			71. The base of boundless consciousness	75. The base of boundless consciousness	3	Y		79. The base of boundless consciousness
			72. The base of nothingness	76. The base of nothingness	3	Y		80. The base of nothingness
			73. The base of neither perception nor non-perception	77. The base of neither perception nor non-perception	3	Y		81. The base of neither perception nor non-perception
Supramundane consciousness	Supramundane [8]		82. The path of stream-entry	86. The fruition of stream-entry	3			
			83. The path of once-returning	87. The fruition of once-returning	3			
			84. The path of non-returning	88. The fruition of non-returning	3			
			85. The path to Arahantship	89. The fruition of Arahantship	3			

Appendix 5: 52 Types of Mental Factors

Mental Factors that Become Common with Others: [Añña Samāna]

*These 13 become moral or immoral according to the type of consciousness in which they occur.

Seven *Universal* Mental Factors

1. Contact: Phassa
2. Feeling: Vedanā
3. Perception: Saññā
4. Volition: Cetanā
5. One-pointedness: Ekaggatā
6. Life faculty: Jīvitindriya
7. Attention: Manasikāra

Six *Occasional* Mental Factors

8. Applied thought: Vitakka
9. Sustained thought: Vicāra
10. Determination: Adhimokkha
11. Energy: Viriya
12. Rapture: Pīti
13. Desire [to act]: Chanda

Unwholesome Mental Factors: [Akusala-cetasikā]

Four *Universal* Unwholesome Mental Factors

14. Delusion: Moha
15. Lack of shame: Ahirika
16. Disregard for consequence: Anottappa
17. Restlessness: Uddhacca

Ten *Occasional* Unwholesome Mental Factors

Three Mental Factors of the Lust-group

18. Lust: Lobha
19. Wrong View: Diṭṭhi
20. Conceit: Māna

Four Mental Factors of the Hatred-group

21. Hatred: Dosa
22. Envy: Issā
23. Miserliness: Macchariya
24. Remorse: Kukkucca

Two Mental Factors Connected to Sloth

25. Sloth: Thīna
26. Torpor: Middha

One Mental Factor Connected to Doubt

27. Doubt: Vicikicchā

Beautiful Mental Factors: [Sobhana-cetasikā]

19 *Universal* Mental Factors

28. Faith: Saddhā
29. Mindfulness: Sati
30. Moral shame: Hirī
31. Regard for consequence: Ottappa
32. Non-lust: Alobha
33. Non-hatred: Adosa
34. Equanimity: Tatramajjhattatā
35. Tranquility of mental body: Kāya passaddhi
36. Tranquility of consciousness: Citta passaddhi

37. Lightness of mental body: Kāya lahutā
38. Lightness of consciousness: Citta lahutā
39. Pliancy of mental body: Kāya mudutā
40. Pliancy of consciousness: Citta mudutā
41. Wieldiness of mental body: Kāya kammaññatā
42. Wieldiness of consciousness: Citta kammaññatā
43. Proficiency of mental body: Kāya pāguññatā
44. Proficiency of consciousness: Citta pāguññatā
45. Rectitude of mental body: Kāya ujukatā
46. Rectitude of consciousness: Citta ujukatā

Six *Universal* Mental Factors

Three Abstinences: Virati

47. Right speech: Sammā vācā
48. Right action: Sammā kammanta
49. Right livelihood: Sammā ājīva

Two Immeasurable: Appamaññā

50. Compassion: Karuṇā
51. Sympathetic joy: Muditā

Non-delusion: Amoha

52. Faculty of wisdom: Paññindriya

Appendix 6: Dependent Origination

Three Lives	12 Links	20 Modes and 4 Groups
Past	1. Ignorance 2. Volitional Formations	5 causes of the past – 1, 2, 8, 9, 10
Present	3. Consciousness 4. Name-and-form 5. Six sense bases 6. Contact 7. Feeling	5 resultants of the present – 3, 4, 5, 6, 7
	8. Craving 9. Clinging 10. Becoming	5 causes of the present – 8, 9, 10, 1, 2
Future	11. Birth [as rebirth] 12. Aging-and-death	5 resultants of the future – 3, 4, 5, 6, 7

Three Connections:

1. The cause of the past and the resultant of the present [Between #2 volitional formations and #3 consciousness]
2. The resultant of the present and the cause of the present [Between #7 feeling and #8 craving]
3. The cause of the present and the resultant of the future [Between #10 becoming and #11 birth, as rebirth]

Three Rounds:

1. The rounds of the defilements [#1 ignorance, #8 craving, #9 clinging]
2. The rounds of the kamma [#2 volitional formations, #10 a portion of becoming]
3. The rounds of the retribution [#3 consciousness through #7 feeling, #10 a portion of becoming, #11 birth, as rebirth, #12 aging-end-death]

Two Causes:

1. Ignorance: the past to present
2. Craving: the present to future

Appendix 7: Seven Stages of Purification and Knowledge of Vipassanā

Seven Purifications	Knowledge of Vipassanā
1. Purification of morality	The fourfold purity of morality
2. Purification of mind	The access-concentration and absorption-concentration
3. Purification of view	The insight of the characteristics of mentality-materiality
4. Purification by overcoming doubt	The knowledge of clearly knowing the cause and condition of mentality-materiality.
5. Purification by knowledge and vision of what is path and not path	1. The knowledge of meditation 2. The knowledge of arising and passing away [weak stage]
6. Purification by knowledge and vision of the way	2. The knowledge of arising and passing away [mature stage] 3. The knowledge of dissolution 4. The knowledge of terror 5. The knowledge of danger 6. The knowledge of disgust 7. The knowledge of desire for deliverance 8. The knowledge of re-observation 9. The knowledge of equanimity about formations 10. The knowledge in conformity
	The change-of-lineage knowledge [This does not belong to the purification.]
7. Purification by knowledge and vision	1. The knowledge of the path 2. The knowledge of the fruit 3. The knowledge of retrospection

Bibliography

[The Ganhwa-Seon and Vipassanā, What is the same and different] Bhikkhu Kakmuk, [Seon-Woo-Do-Ryang] Vol. 3, 2003

[Translation of the Diamond Sutra with Explanatory Notes] Bhikkhu Kakmuk, [Bul-Kwang-Sha Publishing] 2001, 9th Printing 2017

[Four Kinds of Mindfulness Training] Bhikkhu Kakmuk, [the Center for Early Buddhist Studies] 2003, Revised Edition 4th Printing 2013

[Mindfulness of In-and-Out Breathing] Bhikkhuni Daerim, [the Center for Early Buddhist Studies] 2004, Revised Edition 4th Printing 2015

[Translation of the Dīgha Nikāya, Vol. 1–3] Bhikkhu Kakmuk, [the Center for Early Buddhist Studies] 2006, 4th Printing 2014

[Translation of the Majjhima Nikāya, Vol. 1–4] Bhikkhuni Daerim, [the Center for Early Buddhist Studies] 2012, 3rd Printing 2016

[Translation of Gotama Buddha by Nakamura Hajime] Kim, Gee-Gyun, [Kim-Young-Sha] 2005

[Translation of The Buddha, A Short Study of His Life and Teaching by Ven. Piyadassi Thera] Kim, Jae-Sung, [Go-Yo-Han-Sori] 1990

[Translation of Introduction to the Buddhism by Mastani Fumio] Lee, Won-Sup, [Hyun-Am-Sha] 2001

[Translation of The Saṁyutta Nikāya, Vol. 1–6] Bhikkhu Kakmuk, [the Center for Early Buddhist Studies] 2009, 3rd Printing 2016

[Translation of The Abhidharma Storehouse Treatise, Vol. 1–4] Kwon, Oh-Min, [Dong-Guk Yuk-Gyung-Won] 2002, 2nd Printing 2007

[The Abhidharma Buddhism] Kwon, Oh-Min, [Min-Jok-Sha] 2003

[Translation of The Abhidhammattha Sangaha, Guidance to the Abhidhamma Manual, Vol. 1–2] Bhikkhuni Daerim and Bhikkhu Kakmuk, [the Center for Early Buddhist Studies] 2002–2015, 12th Printing, Revised Edition 2017

[Translation of the Āgama Sutras by Mastani Fumio] Lee, Won-Sup, 1976, 22nd Printing 1997

[Translation of The Aṅguttara Nikāya, Vol. 1–6] Bhikkhuni Daerim, [the Center for Early Buddhist Studies] 2006–2007, 3rd Printing 2016

[Translation of Vedanā-Saṁyutta, Contemplation of Feeling, The Discourse-Grouping on the Feelings] Bhikkhuni Daerim, [Go-Yo-Han-Sori] 1996

[Translation of The Upanishads, Vol. 1–2] Lee, Jae-Sook, [Han-Gil-Sha] 1996

[Translation of A Study of the Vinaya-Piṭaka by Nakamura Hajime] Park, Yong-Gil, [To-Bang] 1995

[Translation of History of the Indian Buddhism by Etienne Lamotte, Vol. 1–2] Bhikkhu Hojin, [Shi-Gong-Sha] 2006

[Translation of History of the Indian Buddhism by Pyung Chun, Chang, Vol. 1–2] Lee, Ho-Gun, [Min-Jok-Sha] 1989, 1991

[Translation of Indian Philosophy by Radhakrishnan, Vol. 1–4] Lee, Gyu-Roung, [Han-Gil-Sha] 1999

[Translation of A Study of the Early Buddhist Order by Sato Mitsuo] Kwon, Oh-Min, [Min-Jok-Sha] 1989

[Understanding Early Buddhism] Bhikkhu Kakmuk, [the Center for Early Buddhist Studies] 2010, 5th Printing 2015

[Translation of the Path of Purification, Visuddhimagga, Vol. 1–3] Bhikkhuni Daerim, [the Center for Early Buddhist Studies] 2004, 6th Printing 2016

[Translation of a Study of the Early Buddhist Order in the Vinaya Piṭaka by Mitsuo, Sato] Kim, Ho-Sung, [Min-Jok-Sha] 1991

[Kanpa-shibu-shiagon-goshōroku] Chizen Akanuma, 1926

[CBETA Electronic Buddhist Dictionary] CD-ROM, Chinese Buddhist Electronic Text Association Taipei, 2008

[A Korean-English Dictionary of Buddhism] A. Charles Muller and Ockbae Chun [Un-Ju-Sha] 2014

[A Pali-English Glossary of Buddhist Technical Terms] Bhikkhu Ñāṇamoli, [the Buddhist Publication Society (BPS), Kandy, Sri Lanka] 1994, 1998

[The Pali Text Society's Pali-English Dictionary] The Pali Text Society London, England [Repressed Publishing LLC] 1921, 2016

[The Abhidhammattha Sangaha, Comprehensive Manual of Abhidhamma] Bhikkhu Bodhi, [the Buddhist Publication Society (BPS), Kandy, Sri Lanka] 1993, 1999

[The Connected Discourses of the Buddha: A Translation of the
    Saṃyutta Nikāya] Bhikkhu Bodhi, [Wisdom Publications] 2000
[The Long Discourses of the Buddha: A Translation of the Dīgha
    Nikāya] Maurice Walshe, [Wisdom Publications] 1987, 1995
[The Middle Length Discourses of the Buddha: A Translation of the
    Majjhima Nikāya] Bhikkhu Ñāṇamoli and Bhikkhu Bodhi, [Wis-
    dom Publications] 1995
[The Numerical Discourses of the Buddha: A Translation of the
    Aṅguttara Nikāya] Bhikkhu Bodhi, [Wisdom Publications] 2012
[A Pali-English Glossary of Buddhist Technical Terms] Bhikkhu
    Ñāṇamoli, [BPS Pariyatti Publishing] 1994, 1998
[Translation of the Dhammapada] F. Max Muller, [Create Space
    Independent Publishing Platform]
[Visuddhimagga: The Path of Purification] Bhikkhu Ñāṇamoli, [the
    Buddhist Publication Society (BPS), Kandy, Sri Lanka] 1999, 2013

Index of Early Buddhist Terms

ABOUT THE AUTHOR
Bhikkhu Kakmuk

In 1957 Bhikkhu Kakmuk was born in the City of Mil-Yang, South Korea. While attending the Busan National University, majoring in mathematics education, he became a monastic. He received Novice ordination as a student of Bhikkhu Dogwang of Hwa-um-sha in 1979. He received Bhikkhu ordination from Bhikkhu Jaun in 1982.

After seven years of meditation at various traditional Seon [meditation] centers in Korea, he hoped to translate Pāli Tipiṭaka into Korean and left for India to study. For the next ten years, he learned Sanskrit, Pāli, and the Prakrits languages, completed a master's degree and PhD in the Sanskrit language at Pune University, India. Currently, he is an instructor at the Center for Early Buddhist Studies and also is a professor at the Education Center of the Jogye Order of Korean Buddhism.

The publications he translated or authored are *Translation of the Diamond Sutra with Explanatory Notes*, 2001–2017, 9th printing, *Translation of the Abhidhammattha Sangaha, Guidance to the Abhidhamma Manual*, Vol. 1–2, 2002–2015, 12th printing, revised edition, 2017, co-translated with Bhikkhuni Daerim, *Four Kinds of Mindfulness Training*, 2003–2013, revised edition, 4th printing, *Translation of the Dīgha Nikāya*, Vol. 1–3, 2006–2014, 4th printing,

Translation of the Saṁyutta Nikāya, Vol. 1–6, 2009–2016, 3rd printing, *Understanding Early Buddhism*, 2010–2015, 5th printing, *the Collection of Selected Suttas from Nikāyas*, Vol. 1–2, 2013–2015, 3rd printing, and *Translation of the Dhammasaṅganī*, Vol. 1–2, 2016. He also authored numerous theses and articles including *The Ganhwa-Seon and Vipassanā, What is the same and different* in Seon-Woo-Do-Ryang, 3rd publication, 2003.

He and Bhikkhuni Daerim received a citation from the head of Jogye Order of Korean Buddhism and the Tenth Daewon Award in 2012 for completing the translation of the four Nikāyas.

Translator's Note

I would like to thank Bhikkhu Kakmuk and Bhikkhuni Daerim of the Center for Early Buddhist Studies for allowing me to translate this book. This has been a truly wonderful learning experience for me. I would like to thank my friend, Mary Grant for devoting many hours for editing this book with me. Bhikkhu Kakmuk was always there to guide me in dealing with technical terms and Pali words. Whenever I struggled with unfamiliar Korean words, I reached out to Ju, Bong Hwan. I also would like to thank my daughter, Sarah Acord for giving me tips on improving the readability of this book. Bhikkhu Kakmuk and Kim, Dae Hwan offered me many helpful suggestions in preliminary drafts of this translation. Ven. Bhikkhu Bodhi read the manuscript and gave me truly wonderful feedback. Thank you all for your encouragement and help!

I became very interested in translating this book for several reasons. First, there are so many books on Buddhism – it can be a daunting task to study this subject! This book is an excellent, comprehensive introduction to Early Buddhism. Second, for those Koreans who struggle with books on Buddhism written in Chinese and want to study Buddhism in English, this is a great source. Third, for those Korean monastics who want to teach Buddhism in English, this makes a great textbook. Fourth, this book touches upon the ongoing struggle to make sense of the relationship between Seon Buddhism of Korea and Early Buddhism. It also makes a connection between Mahāyāna Buddhism and Early Buddhism. In short, this is an excellent book for anyone – from beginner to teacher – who wants to learn or teach Early Buddhism.

In translating this book, I try to avoid redundant translations such as Pāli to Korean to English. Since there are many excellent translations from Pāli to English already, I used them whenever I can. For suttas, I used translations by Bhikkhu Bodhi, Bhikkhu Ñāṇamoli, Maurice Walshe, and F. Max Muller. I also used the Visuddhimagga – a translation by Bhikkhu Ñāṇamoli and the Abhidhammattha Sangaha – a translation by Bhikkhu Bodhi. For dictionaries, I used *A Pali-English Glossary of Buddhist Technical Terms* by Bhikkhu Ñāṇamoli, *The Pali-English Dictionary* by the Pali Text Society, and *A Korean-English Dictionary of Buddhism* by A. Charles Muller and Ockbae Chun. Many thanks to aforementioned translators, authors, and publishers for letting me use their books.

There are many technical Buddhist terms in various languages [Chinese, English, Korean, Pāli, and Sanskrit] presented in this book. Since this can be confusing for the readers, I tried to use a consistent translation of these terms. As a result, at times, I modified few words in the excerpts to maintain consistency throughout the book.

Again, thank you and may you always be happy!

TRANSLATOR

Nancy Acord [a.k.a. Sohn, Dong Ran] was born in Seoul, Korea in 1957 and moved to the United States in 1976. After completing her bachelor's degree in business administration at California State University in Los Angeles, she worked as a Certified Public Accountant for international accounting firms and as a Chief Financial Officer and Chief Executive Officer at a US national healthcare organization. Since retiring from her business career in 2004, she has devoted herself to Buddhist studies. In 2014, she founded the Nibbana Buddhist Education Foundation in the United States.

EDITOR

Mary Garcia Grant started her writing career as a typesetter, proofreader, copy editor and journalist for the Emporia Gazette, the American newspaper brought to prominence by the Pulitzer Prize-winning writer William Allen White in Emporia, Kansas. Later she worked at NASA's Goddard Institute for Space Studies in New York City as an editing assistant to scientists who researched global climate change. Her primary study was in violin performance at Rice University in Houston and the City University of New York at Queens College. She has been a violinist with the Kansas City Symphony for 30 years but still enjoys writing and editing.

Made in the USA
Monee, IL
30 September 2022

14978168R00132